POPULAR WILDFLOWERS

of South-Central

British

Columbia

NEIL L. JENNINGS

RMB

This book is dedicated to my children,
Shawn, Jenise, Matthew and Simon,
all of whom put up with my wildflower passion,
often even aiding and abetting it. Thanks for that. I
am enormously proud of each of you.

Popular Wildflowers of South-Central British Columbia
Copyright © 2020 by Neil L. Jennings
First Edition

For information on purchasing bulk quantities of this book, or to
obtain media excerpts or invite the author to speak at an event,
please visit rmbooks.com and select the "Contact" tab.

RMB | Rocky Mountain Books Ltd.
rmbooks.com
@rmbooks
facebook.com/rmbooks

Cataloguing data available from Library and Archives Canada
ISBN 9781771603478 (paperback)
ISBN 9781771603485 (electronic)

All photographs are by the author unless otherwise noted.

Printed and bound in Canada

We would like to also take this opportunity to acknowledge the traditional territories
upon which we live and work. In Calgary, Alberta, we acknowledge the Niitsitapi
(Blackfoot) and the people of the Treaty 7 region in Southern Alberta, which includes
the Siksika, the Piikuni, the Kainai, the Tsuut'ina and the Stoney Nakoda First Nations,
including Chiniki, Bearpaw, and Wesley First Nations. The City of Calgary is also home
to Métis Nation of Alberta, Region III. In Victoria, British Columbia, we acknowledge the
traditional territories of the Lkwungen (Esquimalt, and Songhees), Malahat, Pacheedaht,
Scia'new, T'Sou-ke and W̱SÁNEĆ (Pauquachin, Tsartlip, Tsawout, Tseycum) peoples.

We acknowledge the financial support of the Government of Canada through the Canada
Book Fund and the Canada Council for the Arts, and of the province of British Columbia
through the British Columbia Arts Council and the Book Publishing Tax Credit.

Disclaimer
It is up to the users of this guidebook to acquire the necessary skills for safe experiences
and to exercise caution. The author and publisher of this guide accept no responsibility for
your actions or the results that occur from another's actions, choices, or judgments. If you
have any doubt as to the safety of any given plant, avoidance is the best course of action.

CONTENTS

ACKNOWLEDGEMENTS

I owe a debt of gratitude to a number of family members who contributed to this book by their continuous encouragement and support. Particular appreciation goes to my wife, Linda, who accompanied me on many flower outings and allowed me frequent absences from other duties in favour of chasing blooming flowers. My children, and, I am happy to say, their children, all deserve mention as well, given that they were often seconded to tramp around with me and bring me home alive. Thanks also go to many friends who encouraged me in my projects and often went into the field with me, according me a level of patience that was above and beyond the call of duty. I also wish to especially thank (or perhaps blame) the now departed S. Don Cahoon, who often shamed me with my ignorance and convinced me to educate myself about the beauty that resides in fields of wildflowers.

INTRODUCTION

This book is intended to be a field guide for the amateur naturalist to the identification of wild flowering plants commonly found in the south central areas of British Columbia. The region covered extends eastward generally from the eastern side of the coastal mountains to the Rocky Mountain trench and includes the northern portions of several of the border states of the USA.

This is not a book for scientists. It is for the curious traveller who wants to become acquainted with the flowers encountered during outings. The book differs from most other field guides in that it makes no assumption that the reader has any background in things botanical. It is also small enough to actually carry in the field and not be a burden. I believe most people want to be able to identify the flowers they encounter, because this enriches their outdoor experience. Some might think it a difficult skill to perfect, but take heart and consider this: you can easily put names and faces together for several hundred family members, friends, acquaintances, movie stars, authors, business and world leaders, sports figures etc. Wildflower recognition is no different, and it need not be complicated.

The book does not cover all of the species of wildflowers and flowering shrubs that exist here, but it does include a large representation of the more common floral communities that might be encountered in a typical day during the blooming season. No book that I am acquainted with covers all species in any region, and indeed if such a source existed, it would be too large to be easily carried. Obviously, space will not permit a discussion of all such species, nor would it be pertinent for the amateur naturalist. The region harbours a vast diversity of habitat. In fact, for its relative size, the region is said to have some of the greatest diversity of plant species of any comparable area in North America.

"Do you know what this flower is called?" is one of the most often asked questions when I meet people in the field. Hopefully, this book will enable the user to answer that question. Identification of the unknown species is based on comparison of the unknown plant with the photographs contained in the book, augmented by the narrative descriptions associated with the species pictured. In many instances the exact species will be apparent, while in other cases the reader will be led to plants that are similar to the unknown plant, thus providing a starting point for further investigation. For the purposes of this book, scientific jargon has been kept to a minimum. I have set out to produce the best photographic representations I could obtain, together with some information about the plant that the reader might find interesting and that might assist the reader in remembering the names of the plants. In my view, what most people really want to know about wildflowers is "what is this thing?" and "tell me something interesting about it." Botanical detail, while interesting and enlightening to some of us, will turn off many people.

The plants depicted in the book are arranged first by colour and then by family. This is a logical arrangement for the non-botanist because the first thing a person notes about a flower is its colour. All of the plants shown in the book are identified by their prevailing common names. Where I knew of other common names applied to any plant, I've noted them. I have also included the scientific names of the plants. This inclusion is made to promote specificity. Common names vary significantly from one geographic region to another, but scientific names do not. If you want to learn the scientific names of the plants to promote precision, that's fine. If not, no worries, but just be mindful that many plants have different common names applied to them depending on geography and local usage.

A few cautionary comments and suggestions:

While you are outdoors, go carefully among the plants so as not to damage or disturb them. Stay on the established trails; those trails exist to allow us to view the natural environment without trampling it to death. Many environments are delicate and can be significantly damaged by indiscriminately tromping around in the flora.

Do not pick the flowers. Leave them for others to enjoy.

Do not attempt to transplant wild plants. Such attempts are most often doomed to failure.

Do not eat any plants or plant parts. Do not attempt to use any plants or plant parts for medicinal purposes. To do so presents a potentially significant health hazard. Many of the plants are poisonous – some violently so.

One final cautionary note: the pursuit of wildflowers can be addictive, though not hazardous to your health.

Neil L. Jennings
Calgary, Alberta

TERRITORIAL RANGE OF WILDFLOWERS

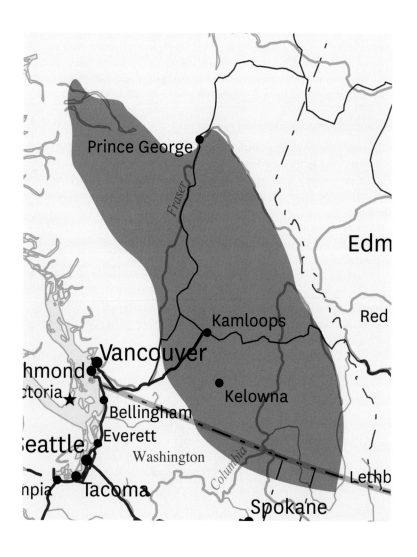

Yellow Flowers

This section includes flowers that are predominantly yellow when encountered in the field, varying from bright yellow to pale cream. Some of the species included here have other colour variations, though, so you might have to check other parts of the book to find the one you're looking for. For example, the Paintbrushes (*Castilleja* sp) have a yellow variation but are most often encountered as red, so they are pictured in that section for purposes of sorting.

Skunk Cabbage (Yellow Arum)

Lysichiton americanum

ARUM FAMILY

This distinctive early-blooming perennial grows in large patches from a fleshy rhizome, and inhabits swamps, bogs, marshes and mucky ground at low to mid-elevations. The inflorescence appears before the leaves do, and consists of hundreds of tiny green-ish-yellow flowers sunk into a thick, fleshy stalk known as a spadix, which is surrounded by a large, bright-yellow sheath leaf called a spathe. The broadly elliptical leaves are huge, growing up to 120 cm long on stout stalks. The whole plant has an earthy odour, giving rise to the common name.

Oregon Grape

Mahonia nervosa

BARBERRY FAMILY

This evergreen shrub is widespread in the foothills, commonly at low to mid-elevations on dry plateaus and in dry to moist forests and openings. The plant very closely resembles holly, with shiny, sharp-pointed leaves that turn to lovely orange and rusty colours in the fall. Its round flowers are pale to bright yellow, and bloom in the early spring, giving way to a small purple berry that resembles a grape.

Common Bladderwort

Utricularia vulgaris

BLADDERWORT FAMILY

This aquatic carnivorous plant is found in shallow water in sloughs, lakes, ditches and ponds. It floats beneath the surface of the water, with a tangle of coarse stems and leaves. The long, branching, submerged stems have finely divided leaves that spread out like little nets. Attached to the leaves hang numerous small bladders that are actually traps for aquatic insects. When an insect swims into a bladder, small hairs are tripped, which shuts the bladder, trapping the insect inside. The insects are then digested, providing a source of nitrogen for the plant.

Blazing Star (Giant Blazing Star)

Mentzelia laevicaulis

BLAZING STAR FAMILY

This spectacular plant grows up to 1 m tall, and occurs in arid basins and dry grasslands from valleys to montane elevations. Stiff, barbed grey hairs cover the angular stems and foliage of the plant. The leaves are up to 30 cm long, lance-shaped and deeply lobed, with wavy margins. The flowers occur at the top of stout, satiny white stems. The lemon-yellow flowers are large and star-like, with five lance-shaped petals up to 8 cm long and numerous long yellow stamens that burst forth in a fountain-like display.

Puccoon (Lemonweed)

Lithospermum ruderale

BORAGE FAMILY

A coarse perennial up to 50 cm tall, this plant is firmly anchored to dry slopes and grasslands by a large woody taproot. Its numerous sharp-pointed leaves are lance-shaped and clasp the stem. The small yellow flowers are partly hidden in the axils of the leaves near the top of the plant, and have a strong, pleasant scent. The stems and leaves are covered in long white hairs. The fruit is an oval, cream-coloured nutlet that is somewhat pitted and resembles pointed teeth.

Yellow Buckwheat (Umbrella Plant)

Eriogonum flavum

BUCKWHEAT FAMILY

This fuzzy-haired tufted perennial favours dry, often sandy or rocky outcrops, eroded slopes and badlands. The leaves are dark green on top, but appear white and felt-like on the underside due to the dense hairs. The yellow flowers occur in compound umbels – umbrella shaped clusters – atop the stem. The common name Umbrella Plant is testimony to the shape of the inflorescence.

Sagebrush Buttercup
Ranunculus glaberrimus

BUTTERCUP FAMILY

This beautiful little buttercup is one of the earliest-blooming wildflowers in the region, with its shiny, bright-yellow petals peeping out from the dead winter grasses of early spring on arid hillsides. The leaves are mainly basal and elliptical to lance-shaped. The flowers appear in patches or as single blooms. Sagebrush Buttercups are poisonous, containing an acrid alkaloid, and some Indigenous peoples warned their children not to touch or pick them.

Yellow Columbine
Aquilegia flavescens

BUTTERCUP FAMILY

Lemon-yellow in colour, these beautiful flowers nod at the ends of slender stems that lift the flowers above the leaves. Each flower is composed of five wing-shaped sepals and five tube-shaped petals that flare at the open end and taper to a distinctive spur at the opposite end. The leaves are mainly basal, with long stems, and are deeply lobed. The plant occurs on rockslides and talus slopes and in meadows in the alpine and subalpine zones.

Brittle Prickly-Pear Cactus

Opuntia fragilis

CACTUS FAMILY

This easily recognized plant is prostrate and can form mats on dry, exposed slopes in eroded areas and badlands, often growing in sandy or rocky soil. The stems are flattened and broad, and are covered with clusters of hard, sharp spines that have tufts of sharp bristles at the base. The flowers are large and showy, with numerous yellow petals that are waxy and up to 5 cm long. The fruits are pear-shaped spiny berries which are edible and are often browsed by antelope.

Narrow-Leaved Desert Parsley (Nine-Leaf Biscuit-Root)

Lomatium triternatum

CARROT FAMILY

This perennial herb occurs in dry to moist open sites from foothills to montane elevations and grows up to 80 cm tall. Its mostly basal leaves are hairy and divided into segments, often in three sets of three leaflets each. The leaf stalks are irregular in length and clasp the stem. The yellow flowers are very small, occurring in compound, flat-topped clusters (umbels) atop the stems. Often there are a few slender, leafy bracts just below the junction of the individual stalks, but no bracts occur at the base of the flower arrangement.

Arrow-Leaved Balsamroot

Balsomorhiza sagittata

COMPOSITE FAMILY

This is a widespread and frequently abundant plant of hot, arid climates, often found on rocky south-facing slopes. Its flowers are solitary composite heads with bright-yellow ray flowers and yellow disc flowers, and are densely hairy, especially at the base. The large, silvery leaves are arrowhead-shaped and covered with dense, felt-like hairs. Balsamroot often provides a showy early-spring splash of colour on warm, dry hillsides. All parts of the plant are edible, and the species was an important food for Indigenous peoples.

Brown-Eyed Susan (Gaillardia)

Gaillardia aristata

COMPOSITE FAMILY

This is a plant of open grasslands, dry hillsides, roadsides and open woods. The flowers are large and showy, with yellow ray florets that are purplish to reddish at the base. The central disc is purplish and woolly hairy. The leaves are numerous, alternate and lance-shaped, usually looking greyish and rough owing to the many short hairs. A number of Indigenous peoples used the plant to relieve a variety of ailments.

Canada Goldenrod

Solidago canadensis

COMPOSITE FAMILY

This upright perennial grows from a creeping rhizome and often forms large colonies in moist soil in meadows and along stream banks and lakeshores. Its solitary flowering stem is up to 1 m tall or more, has many branches near the top and is covered with short, dense hairs. The simple, alternate leaves – all on the stem and relatively uniform in size – are lance-shaped to linear, sharply saw-toothed, and hairy. The tiny yellow flowers occur in dense, pyramid-shaped clusters at the tops of the stem branches. Each flower has yellow ray and disc florets.

Curly-Cup Gumweed

Grindelia squarrosa

COMPOSITE FAMILY

This plant is a sticky perennial or biennial that grows up to 1 m tall from a deep taproot, and occurs on roadsides, saline flats, slough margins and dry grasslands. Its leaves are dark green, narrowly oblong, entire or slightly toothed, and glandular-sticky. The lower leaves have long stalks, while the upper ones are stalkless and somewhat clasping, with pointed or rounded tips. The flowers appear as numerous heads, with bright-yellow ray florets.

Goat's-Beard (Yellow Salsify)

Tragopogon dubius

COMPOSITE FAMILY

A plant of grasslands, roadsides, ditches and dry waste areas, Goat's-Beard was introduced from Europe. Its yellow flower is a large, solitary, erect head surrounded by long, narrow, protruding green bracts. The leaves are alternate, fleshy and narrow, but broad and clasping at the base. The fruit, a mass of white, narrow-ribbed, beaked achenes, resembles the seed pod of a common dandelion, but is significantly larger, approaching the size of a softball. The flowers open on sunny mornings, but then close up around noon and stay closed for the rest of the day.

Heart-Leaved Arnica

Arnica cordifolia

COMPOSITE FAMILY

Arnica is a common plant of wooded areas in the mountains, foothills and boreal forest. The leaves occur in two to four opposite pairs along the stem, each with long stalks and heart-shaped, serrated blades. The uppermost pair is stalkless and more lance-shaped than the lower leaves. The flowers have 10–15 bright-yellow ray florets and bright-yellow central disc florets.

Pineapple Weed (Disc Mayweed)

Matricaria discoidea

COMPOSITE FAMILY

This branching annual grows up to 40 cm tall along roadsides, in ditches and on disturbed ground. The stem leaves are alternate and fern-like, with finely dissected, narrow segments. Basal leaves have usually fallen off by the time flowering occurs. The flowers are several to many composite heads, with greenish to yellow disc florets on a cone- or dome-shaped base. There are no ray florets. When crushed, the leaves and flowers of the plant produce a distinctive pineapple aroma, hence the common name.

Sow Thistle (Perennial Sow Thistle)

Sonchus arvensis

COMPOSITE FAMILY

This is a plant of cultivated fields, roadsides, ditches and pastures. The flowers have large yellow ray florets similar to dandelion flowers. Sow Thistle is an imported species from Europe and is not a true thistle. Sow Thistles will exude a milky latex when the stem is crushed, while true thistles do not. The common name is derived from the fact that pigs like to eat this plant.

Spear-Head Senecio (Arrow-Leaved Ragwort)

Senecio triangularis

COMPOSITE FAMILY

This leafy, lush perennial herb often grows to 150 cm tall and occurs in large clumps in moist to wet open or partly shaded sites from foothills to alpine elevations. The leaves are alternate, spearhead or arrow-head-shaped, squared off at the base and tapered to a point. The leaves are numerous and well developed along the whole stem. The flowers occur in flat-topped clusters at the top of the plant and have five to eight bright-yellow ray florets surrounding a disc of bright-yellow to orange florets.

Tansy

Tanacetum vulgare

COMPOSITE FAMILY

This plant was introduced from Europe and is common in pastures and disturbed areas and along roadsides, embankments and fences. Its flattened yellow flowers occur in numerous bunches atop multiple stalks and resemble buttons. The dark-green, finely dissected leaves are fern-like and strong smelling. During the Middle Ages a posy of Tansy was thought, fancifully, to ward off the Black Death.

Woolly Groundsel (Woolly Ragwort)

Senecio canus

COMPOSITE FAMILY

This perennial grows from a woody stem base and taproot, with erect stems that are white woolly and grow to 40 cm tall. The plant grows in dry areas, from open rocky or sandy places in sagebrush flats to the alpine zone. The whole plant has a silvery appearance owing to the woolly hairs. The basal leaves and lower stem leaves are elliptical, stalked and white woolly-hairy. The middle and upper leaves are alternate and become sessile. The rounded inflorescence consists of composite heads with woolly bases and yellow ray and disc flowers.

Yellow Evening Primrose

Oenothera villosa (also *O. strigosa*)

EVENING PRIMROSE FAMILY

An erect, robust, leafy biennial, this plant forms a rosette of leaves the first year, and puts up a tall, leafy stem the second. The flowers have large, bright-yellow, cross-shaped stigma, with numerous yellow stamens. The flowers usually open in the evening and fade in the morning, a behaviour adopted because moths are the principal pollinators of the plant. The plant gets its common name from its habit of blooming at dusk.

Bracted Lousewort (Wood Betony)

Pedicularis bracteosa

FIGWORT FAMILY

This plant can attain heights of up to 1 m, and is found at subalpine and alpine elevations in moist forests, meadows and clearings. Its fern-like leaves are divided into long, narrow, toothed segments and are attached to the upper portions of the stem of the plant. The flowers, varying from yellow to red to purple, arise from the axils of leafy bracts and occur in an elongated cluster at the top of the stem. They have a two-lipped corolla, giving the impression of a bird's beak.

Butter and Eggs (Toadflax)

Linaria vulgaris

FIGWORT FAMILY

This is a common plant of roadsides, ditches, fields and disturbed areas that grows to 1 m tall. Its dark-green leaves are alternate and narrow. The bright-yellow, orange throated flowers are similar in shape to Snapdragons and occur in dense terminal clusters at the tops of erect stems. The corolla is spurred at the base and two-lipped, the upper lip having two lobes, the lower one, three. The common name arises from the yellow and orange tones on the flowers, reminiscent of butter and eggs.

Common Mullein
Verbascum thapsis

FIGWORT FAMILY

This Eurasian import is quite common along roadsides, in gravelly places and on dry slopes. The plant is a biennial, taking two years to produce flowers. In the first year, it puts out a rosette of large leaves that are very soft to the touch, much like velvet or flannel. A strong, sentinel-like stalk appears in the second year. The small yellow flowers appear randomly on the flowering spike. At no time do all the flowers bloom together. After flowering the dead stalk turns dark brown and may persist for many months.

Yellow Monkeyflower
Mimulus guttatus

FIGWORT FAMILY

This plant occurs, often in large patches, along streams, at seeps and in moist meadows. The species is quite variable, but is always spectacular when found. The bright-yellow flowers resemble Snapdragons, and occur in clusters. They usually have red or purple dots on the lip, giving the appearance of a grinning face. The genus name, *Mimulus*, is derived from the Latin *mimus*, which means "mimic" or "actor."

Yellow Beardtongue (Yellow Penstemon)

Penstemon confertus

FIGWORT FAMILY

This is a plant of moist to dry meadows, woodlands, stream banks, hillsides and mountains. The small, pale-yellow flowers are numerous, and appear in whorled, interrupted clusters along the upper part of the stem. Each flower is tube-shaped and has two lips. The lower lip is three-lobed and bearded at the throat, while the upper one is two-lobed. The common name, Beardtongue, describes the hairy, tongue-like staminode (sterile stamen) in the throat of the flower. The genus name, *Penstemon*, is a reference to the five stamens in the flower

Golden Corydalis

Corydalis aurea

FUMITORY FAMILY

This plant of open woods, roadsides, disturbed places and stream banks is an erect or spreading, branched, leafy biennial or annual. It germinates in the fall and overwinters as a seedling. In the spring it grows rapidly, flowers, and then dies. The yellow flowers are irregularly shaped, rather like the flowers of the pea family, with keels at the tips. A long, nectar-producing spur extends backward from the upper petal.

Black Twinberry (Bracted Honeysuckle)

Lonicera involucrata

HONEYSUCKLE FAMILY

This plant is a shrub that grows up to 2 m tall in moist woods and along stream banks. Its yellow flowers occur in pairs arising from the axils of the leaves, and are overlain by a purple to reddish leafy bract. As the fruit ripens the bract remains, enlarges and darkens in colour. The ripe fruits occur in pairs and are black. They are bitter to the taste, but serve as food for a variety of birds and small mammals.

Glacier Lily (Yellow Avalanche Lily)

Erythronium grandiflorum

LILY FAMILY

This gorgeous lily is one of the first blooms in the spring, often appearing at the edges of receding snowbanks on mountain slopes, thus the common names. The bright-yellow flowers that appear at the top of the leafless stem are usually solitary, though a plant might have up to three flowers. The flowers are nodding, with six tepals that are tapered to the tip and reflexed, with white, yellow or brown anthers. The broadly oblong, glossy leaves, usually two, are attached near the base of the stem and are unmarked.

Yellowbell

Fritillaria pudica

LILY FAMILY

This diminutive flower is a harbinger of spring, often blooming just after snowmelt in dry grasslands and dry, open ponderosa pine forests. It can easily be overlooked because of its small size, usually standing only about 15 cm tall. The yellow, drooping, bell-shaped flowers are very distinctive. The flowers turn orange to brick red as they age. The leaves, usually two or three, are linear to lance-shaped, and appear more or less opposite about halfway up the stem. The Yellowbell sometimes appears with two flowers on a stem, but single blooms are more common.

Douglas Maple (Rocky Mountain Maple)

Acer glabrum

MAPLE FAMILY

This deciduous shrub or small tree is found in moist, sheltered sites from foothills to subalpine zones. The plant has graceful, wide-spreading branches. The young twigs are smooth and cherry-red, turning grey with age. The leaves are opposite and typical of maples: three-lobed, with an unequal and sharply toothed margin. The yellowish-green flowers are short-lived and fragrant, with five petals and five sepals, hanging in loose clusters. The fruits are v-shaped pairs of winged seeds joined at the point of attachment to the shrub. The fruit is known as a "samara."

Golden Draba (Yellow Draba, Golden Whitlow Grass)

Draba aurea

MUSTARD FAMILY

This mustard grows up to 50 cm tall, and occurs on rocky slopes and in open woods and meadows from the montane to the alpine zones. Its hairy basal leaves are lance-shaped and appear in a rosette. The stalkless, hairy, lance-shaped stem leaves are alternate, somewhat clasping, and distributed up the stem. The bright-yellow flowers are four-petalled and appear in a cluster at the top of the stem. Mustards typically have four petals in a cruciform shape.

Prairie Rocket

Erysimum asperum

MUSTARD FAMILY

This erect, robust plant grows to 50 cm tall or more in dry, sandy grasslands, particularly in the southeastern parts of the region. The bright-yellow flowers appear in rounded clusters at the terminal ends of stout branching stems. The stem leaves are simple, alternate and lance-shaped. At one time, children were treated for worms with a concoction made from the crushed seeds of this plant mixed in water.

Soopolallie (Canadian Buffaloberry)

Shepherdia canadensis

OLEASTER FAMILY

This deciduous shrub can reach 3 m tall, and is often the dominant understorey cover in lodgepole pine forests. All parts of the plant are covered with shiny, rust-coloured scales, giving the whole plant an orange, rusty appearance. The leaves are leathery and thick, green and glossy on the upper surface, while the lower surface is covered with white hairs and sprinkled with rusty-coloured dots. The male and female flowers appear on separate plants. The small, inconspicuous yellow flowers often appear on the branches of the plant before the arrival of the leaves.

Wolf Willow (Silverberry)

Elaeagnus commutata

OLEASTER FAMILY

Another tall deciduous shrub, growing to 4 m, often in dense stands. Its twigs are thickly covered with rusty-brown scales, while its oval, silvery leaves are alternate and similarly covered with small scales. The flowers are funnel-shaped and have four yellow lobes, occurring at the leaf axils. The flowers are very fragrant with a distinctive aroma. The fruits are silvery, round to egg-shaped berries that usually persist throughout the winter.

Yellow Lady's Slipper

Cypripedium parviflorum

ORCHID FAMILY

This is an orchid of bogs, damp woods and stream banks. Its leaves are alternate, broadly elliptical and clasping, with two to four per stem. The yellow flowers usually occur singly on a stem, and resemble a small shoe. The sepals and lateral petals are similar, greenish-yellow to brownish, and have twisted, wavy margins. The lower petal forms a prominent pouch-shaped yellow lip with purple dotting around the puckered opening. This flower has suffered large range reductions as a result of picking and attempted transplantation, which almost always fails.

Field Locoweed

Oxytropis campestris

PEA FAMILY

This early-blooming plant is widespread and common among rocky outcrops, along roadsides and in dry open woods. Its leaves are mainly basal, with elliptical leaflets and dense hairs. The pale-yellow, pea-like flowers bloom in clusters at the top of a leafless, hairy stem. The plant is poisonous to cattle, sheep and horses, owing to its high content of alkaloids that cause blind staggers. This loss of muscle control in animals that have ingested the plant is the origin of the common name for the flower, *loco* being Spanish for "crazy" or "foolish."

Sulphur Lupine

Lupinus sulphureus

PEA FAMILY

This species is a slender, erect, mostly unbranched plant that is stiff-hairy and grows up to 80 cm tall in grasslands and dry open ponderosa forests at low to mid-elevations. Its sharp-pointed leaves are alternate, mostly on the stem, palmately compound and have 8–13 leaflets. The few basal leaves have longer stalks and are hairy on both surfaces. The yellow (sometimes white), pea-like flowers are hairy and whorled or scattered in a raceme along the upper part of the stem.

Yellow Hedysarum

Hedysarum sulphurescens

PEA FAMILY

This is a plant of stream banks, grasslands, open forests and clearings. Its yellowish to nearly white flowers are pea-like and drooping, usually appearing along one side of the stem in elongated clusters (racemes). The fruits of the plant are long, flat, pendulous pods with conspicuous winged edges and constrictions between each of the seeds. This plant is also called Yellow Sweet Vetch. It is an extremely important food for grizzly bears, which eat the roots in the spring and fall.

Yellow Mountain Avens (Drummond's Mountain Avens)

Dryas drummondii

ROSE FAMILY

This is a plant of gravelly streams and riverbanks, slopes and roadsides in foothills and mountains. Its yellow flower is solitary and nodding, with black glandular hairs blooming on the top of a hairy, leafless stalk. Leaves are alternate, leathery and wrinkly, dark green above and whitish-hairy beneath. The fruit consists of many achenes, each with a silky, feathery, golden-yellow plume that becomes twisted around the others into a tight spiral that later opens into a fluffy mass, dispersing the seeds on the wind.

Large-Leaved Avens

Geum macrophyllum

ROSE FAMILY

This is a tall, erect, hairy perennial that grows in moist woods, along rivers and streams and in thickets from low to subalpine elevations. Its bright-yellow flowers are saucer-shaped, with five petals, usually appearing at the tip of a tall, slender stem. The basal leaves occur in a cluster. The terminal leaf is rounded, shallowly lobed and much larger than the lateral leaves below. The fruits are achenes that have hooks on them which will cling to the clothing of passersby and the fur of animals as a seed dispersal mechanism.

Shrubby Cinquefoil
Potentilla fruticosa

ROSE FAMILY

This low deciduous shrub is found on rocky slopes and in dry meadows and gravelly river courses at low to subalpine elevations. Its leaves are alternate, divided into three to seven (usually five) greyish-green leaflets that are lightly hairy and often have curled edges. The flowers are golden yellow and saucer-shaped, with five rounded petals, usually blooming as a solitary at the ends of branches. The flowers are often smaller and paler at lower elevations, larger and brighter in higher terrain. Many *Potentilla* species have five leaflets, and their flower parts are in fives.

Silverweed
Potentilla anserina

ROSE FAMILY

This plant is a low, prostrate perennial that grows from thick rootstock and reddish-coloured runners in moist meadows and on riverbanks, lakeshores and slough margins. Its leaves are basal, compound, toothed and pinnate, with 7–25 leaflets per leaf. Each silky-haired leaflet is green to silvery on top and lighter underneath. The flowers are bright yellow and solitary on leafless stems, with rounded petals in fives. The sepals are light green and hairy, and appear between the petals.

Sticky Cinquefoil
Potentilla glandulosa

ROSE FAMILY

This plant inhabits open forests and meadows at low to mid-elevations, growing to about 40 cm tall from a branched rootstock. Its leaves and stems are covered with glandular hairs that exude a sticky aromatic fluid. The leaves are mainly basal and pinnately divided into five to nine sharp-toothed oval leaflets. The flowers are typical of the *Potentillas,* and are pale yellow to creamy white, occurring in small, open clusters at the tops of the stems.

Yellow Mountain Saxifrage
Saxifraga aizoides

SAXIFRAGE FAMILY

This is a sturdy, ground-hugging perennial that forms loose mats or cushions on moist sand, gravel, stream banks and stones in the alpine zone. Its upright stems can grow to 10 cm tall, and are crowded with fat, succulent, linear leaves that have an abrupt tip. The leaves are covered in very small, pale hairs. The flowers appear at the tops of the stems, pale yellow and often spotted with orange. The flowers have five petals, which may be ragged at the tips. There are 10 stamens with conspicuously large anthers.

Western St. John's Wort

Hypericum scouleri
(also *H. formosum*)

ST. JOHN'S WORT FAMILY

This perennial appears in moist places from foothills to the alpine zone and grows to 25 cm tall. Its leaves are opposite, egg-shaped to elliptical, 1–3 cm long, somewhat clasping at the base, and usually have purplish-black dots along their edges. The bright-yellow flowers have five petals and occur in open clusters at the top of the plant. The stamens are numerous, often resembling a starburst.

Lance-Leaved Stonecrop (Spearleaf Stonecrop)

Sedum lanceolatum

STONECROP FAMILY

This fleshy perennial with reddish stems grows up to 15 cm tall on dry, rocky, open slopes and in meadows and rock crevices from low elevations to above timberline. Its numerous fleshy, alternate leaves are round in cross-section, overlapping and mostly basal. The bright-yellow flowers are star-shaped with sharp-pointed petals, and occur in dense, flat-topped clusters atop short stems.

Round-Leaved Violet (Evergreen Violet)

Viola orbiculata

VIOLET FAMILY

This diminutive flower is an early bloomer, appearing right after the melting snows in moist coniferous forests. Its oval to nearly circular leaves lie flat on the ground and often remain green through the winter. The species name, *orbiculata*, is a reference to the shape of the leaves. The flowers are lemon yellow and have purplish pencilling on the lower three petals. The markings direct insects to the source of the nectar. Candied flowers of this plant are often used for decorating cakes and pastries.

Yellow Wood Violet

Viola glabella

VIOLET FAMILY

This beautiful yellow violet occurs in moist woods, often in extensive patches. There are smooth, serrate, heart-shaped leaves on the upper part of the plant stem. The flowers have very short spurs, and the interior of the side petals often exhibits a white beard. The flower is also commonly referred to as Smooth Violet and Stream Violet.

Blue *and* Purple Flowers

This section includes flowers that are predominantly blue or purple when encountered in the field, ranging from pale blue to deep purple and from light violet to lavender. Some of the lighter hues of blue and purple might shade into pinks, so if you do not find the flower your are looking for here, check the other sections of this book.

Common Butterwort
Pinguicula vulgaris

BLADDERWORT FAMILY

This small plant is one of only a few carnivorous ones in the region. It grows from fibrous roots in bogs, seeps and wetlands and along stream banks and lakeshores from valleys to the subalpine zone. Its pale-green to yellowish leaves are basal, short-stalked, somewhat overlapping and curled in at the margins, forming a rosette on the ground. The leaves have glandular hairs on their upper surface that exude a sticky substance that attracts and then ensnares small insects. The flower is pale to dark purple and solitary atop a leafless stem.

Alpine Forget-Me-Not
Myosotis alpestris

BORAGE FAMILY

This beautiful, fragrant little flower is easily recognized by its wheel-shaped blue corolla and prominent yellow eye. It occurs, often in clumps, in moist subalpine and alpine meadows. Its leaves are lance-shaped to linear, the lower ones having short stems, while the upper ones are clasping. The stems are covered with long, soft hairs. The Alpine Forget-Me-Not is the state flower of Alaska.

Blueweed
(Viper's Bugloss)

Echium vulgare

BORAGE FAMILY

This European import grows up to 80 cm tall and is found along road-sides and in pastures and disturbed areas throughout Canada. It was first introduced as a garden orna-mental, but it escaped and is now a problem weed, forcing out indigen-ous vegetation. The flowers are dis-tributed up a stout central stalk that is hairy in appearance. The flowers are a spectacular bright blue, funnel-shaped, with unequal lobes. The fruits are rough nutlets that are said to resemble a viper's head. The bristly hairs on the leaves and stem of the plant cause severe skin irritation in many people.

Stickseed

Hackelia floribunda

BORAGE FAMILY

This hairy biennial or short-lived perennial has stiffly erect stems and grows to 1 m tall. The small, yellow-centred blue flowers occur in loose clusters on curving stalks near the top of the plant. The fruits are nutlets that are keeled in the middle and attached to a pyra-mid-shaped base. Each nutlet has rows of barbed prickles. While the flowers on this plant are lovely to look at, the prickles on the nutlets cling easily to fur, feathers and clothing, thus lending the plant its common name.

Tall Bluebells
(Tall Lungwort)

Mertensia paniculata

BORAGE FAMILY

This usually hairy perennial can have multiple branches, and grows up to 80 cm tall from a woody rootstock. The plant prefers moist woods, stream banks, shaded poplar groves and mixed forests. Its large, heart-shaped basal leaves are prominently veined, white-hairy on both sides and long-stalked. The stem leaves are stalkless or short-stalked, rounded at the base and tapering to the pointed tip. The blue flowers occur in drooping clusters, hanging like small blue bells. The flower buds often have a pinkish tinge, turning blue as they open.

Blue Clematis

Clematis occidentalis

BUTTERCUP FAMILY

A plant of shaded riverine woods and thickets, the Clematis is a climbing, slightly hairy, reddish-stemmed vine that attaches itself to other plants by slender tendrils. Its flowers have four to five sepals and are purplish to blue in colour, with dark veins. The flowers resemble crepe paper. The fruits are mop-like clusters of seeds, each of which has a long, feathery style. The Blackfoot called the plant "ghost's lariat," a reference to the fact that the vine would entangle their feet when they walked through it. Clematis often goes by the locally common name of Virgin's Bower.

Low Larkspur

Delphinium bicolor

BUTTERCUP FAMILY

This is a plant of open woods, grass-lands and slopes that grows up to 40 cm tall from fleshy rootstock. It usually has a single flowering stem. Larkspurs are easily recognized for their showy, highly modified flowers. The irregular petals are whitish to bluish, with sepals that are blue to violet. The upper sepal forms a large, hollow, nectar-producing spur. The flowers bloom up the stem in a loose, elongated cluster. The common name is said to have originated because the spur on the flower resembles the spur on the foot of a lark. The plant is poisonous to cattle and humans.

Monkshood

Aconitum columbianum

BUTTERCUP FAMILY

A plant of moist mixed coniferous forests and meadows, Monkshood has a distinctive flower construction that is unmistakable. The dark-blue to purple flowers appear in terminal open clusters, and the sepals form a hood like those worn by monks. The long-stalked leaves are alternate and shaped like large maple leaves. The plant contains poisonous alkaloids that can cause death within a few hours.

Prairie Crocus

Anemone patens
(also *Pulsatilla patens*)

BUTTERCUP FAMILY

This plant is widespread and common in grasslands, dry meadows and mountain slopes. It is usually one of the first wildflowers to bloom in the spring, and can occur in huge numbers. Its cup-shaped flowers are usually solitary and in colours from various blues to purples. White varieties also are sometimes seen. It is interesting to note that the flower blooms before the basal leaves appear. The plant has many basal leaves, palmately divided into three main leaflets and again divided into narrow linear segments. The leaves on the flower stem appear in a whorl of three.

Blue Lettuce

Lactuca tatarica
ssp. *pulchella*

COMPOSITE FAMILY

This plant grows up to 1 m tall in fields and meadows and along roadsides, lakeshores and stream banks, often in moist, heavy soil. The leaves are hairless, lobed below and simple above. The flowers are composite heads and have pale to dark-blue ray florets that are toothed at the tip. There are no disc florets.

Blue Sailors (Chicory)
Cichorium intybus

COMPOSITE FAMILY

This native of Eurasia grows up to 175 cm tall at low elevations on dry plateaus and in fields, grasslands and waste areas. Its basal leaves are lance-shaped and strongly toothed to lobed. The flowers have sky-blue ray flowers and no disc flowers, and they occur singly or in small groups widely spaced on the long branches. The flowers open only in the daylight. The stems exude a bitter-tasting, milky juice when broken.

Showy Aster
Aster conspicuus

COMPOSITE FAMILY

This plant is widespread and common in low to mid-elevations in moist to dry open forests, openings, clearings and meadows. The flowers are few to many composite heads on glandular stalks, with 15–35 violet ray flowers and yellow disc flowers. The stem leaves are egg-shaped to elliptical, with sharp-toothed edges and clasping bases. Some Indigenous peoples soaked the roots of the plant in water and used the decoction to treat boils. The leaves were also used as a poultice for that purpose.

Tall Purple Fleabane

Erigeron peregrinus

COMPOSITE FAMILY

This plant grows up to 70 cm tall from a thick rootstock in the subalpine and alpine zones. Its basal leaves are narrow and stemmed, while the stem leaves are smaller and stalkless. The flowers resemble daisies, with 30–80 rose- to purple-coloured ray florets surrounding a yellow centre of disc florets. The large flowers are usually solitary, but there may be smaller ones that appear from the axils of the upper leaves.

Alpine Speedwell (Alpine Veronica)

Veronica wormskjoldii (also *V. alpina*)

FIGWORT FAMILY

This erect perennial stands up to 30 cm tall, and occurs in moist meadows and along streams in the subalpine and alpine zones. Its leaves are elliptical to egg-shaped, and occur in opposite pairs spaced along the stem. The stems, leaves and stalks of the flowers are covered with fine, sticky hairs. The flowers are numerous and occur at the top of the stem. The corolla has four united blue petals, which exhibit dark veins.

Fuzzy-Tongued Penstemon (Shrubby Penstemon)

Penstemon eriantherus

FIGWORT FAMILY

This perennial grows up to 40 cm tall from a taproot on dry open slopes from valleys to the montane zone, and is generally restricted to the southeastern part of the region. The plant is grey-hairy overall. Its basal and lower stem leaves are opposite, usually entire, lance- to egg-shaped and stalked. The upper leaves are lance-shaped to oblong and more or less unstalked. The inflorescence is a terminal cluster of several whorls of stalked, tubular flowers that flare at the mouth. The flowers are pale lavender to blue-purple, with lines of a darker colour inside.

Small-Flowered Penstemon (Slender Beardtongue)

Penstemon procerus

FIGWORT FAMILY

This plant grows up to 40 cm tall at low to alpine elevations, usually in dry to moist open forests, grassy clearings, meadows and disturbed areas. Most of the blunt to lance-shaped leaves appear in opposite pairs up the stem. The small blue to purple flowers are funnel-shaped and appear in one to several tight clusters arranged in whorls around the stem and at its tip. The common name, Beardtongue, describes the hairy, tongue-like staminode in the throat of the flower

Blue Flax

Linum lewisii

FLAX FAMILY

This perennial grows up to 60 cm tall from a woody base and taproot, in grasslands, along roadsides and on dry, exposed hillsides and gravelly river flats. The leaves are alternate, simple and stalkless. The pale, purplish-blue flowers have five petals, five sepals, five styles and five stamens, with darkish guidelines, and are yellowish at the base. They appear on very slender stems that are constantly moving, even with the smallest of breezes. Some Indigenous peoples used the stem fibres in making cordage. The common name, Flax, is derived from the Latin *filum*, which means "thread."

Northern Gentian

Gentianella amarella
(also *Gentiana amarella*)

GENTIAN FAMILY

This plant is found in moist places in meadows, woods and ditches and along stream banks up to the subalpine zone. The flowers are first sighted by their star-like formation winking at the top of the corolla tube, amidst adjacent grasses. The plant is most often small, standing only 15–20 cm. The flowers appear in clusters in the axils of the upper stem leaves, the leaves being opposite and appearing almost to be small hands holding up the flowers for inspection. There is a fringe inside the throat of the flower.

Sticky Purple Geranium
Geranium viscosissimum

GERANIUM FAMILY

This is a plant of moist grasslands, open woods and thickets that can grow up to 60 cm tall. The flowers have large, showy, rose-purple to bluish petals that are strongly veined with purple. The long-stalked leaves are deeply lobed and split into five to seven sharp-toothed divisions, appearing in opposite pairs along the stem. There are sticky glandular hairs covering the stems, leaves and some flower parts. The fruit is an elongated, glandular hairy capsule with a long beak shaped like a stork's or crane's bill.

Harebell
Campanula rotundifolia

HAREBELL FAMILY

This plant is widespread in a variety of habitats, including grasslands, gullies, moist forests, clearings and rocky open ground. The bell-shaped flowers are purplish-blue with hairless sepals, nodding on a thin stem in loose clusters. The leaves are lance-shaped and thin on the stem. The heart-shaped basal leaves are coarse-toothed and usually wither before the flowers appear. *Campanula* is Latin meaning "little bell."

Blue-Eyed Grass

Sisyrinchium angustifolium

IRIS FAMILY

These beautiful flowers can be found scattered among the grasses of moist meadows from low to sub-alpine elevations. Their distinctively flattened stems grow to 30 cm, twice as tall as the grass-like basal leaves. The blue flower is star-shaped, with three virtually identical petals and sepals, each tipped with a minute point. There is a bright-yellow eye in the centre of the flower. The blossoms are very short-lived, wilting usually within a day, to be replaced by fresh ones the next day.

Chocolate Lily (Checker Lily)

Fritillaria affinis

LILY FAMILY

This early-blooming upright perennial grows up to 80 cm tall in variable habitat that includes prairies, grassy bluffs, woodlands and conifer forests from sea level to the montane zone. The plant grows from a cluster of bulbs and small offsets that resemble grains of rice. The narrow, lance-shaped leaves are all borne on the stem, mostly arranged in one or two imperfect whorls of three to five leaves. Several foul-smelling nodding flowers occur in a loose raceme up the stem. Each individual flower has six purple tepals checked with yellow, giving the flower a dark-brown appearance.

Early Camas

Camassia quamash

LILY FAMILY

This plant of wet meadows and stream banks has long, narrow, grass-like leaves and a tall, naked stem. Its startling blue to purplish flowers are numerous and appear in a loose cluster at the top of the stem. The flowers have six tepals that are spreading and somewhat unevenly spaced. The stamens are golden, and contrast vividly with the blue inflorescence of the plant. The bulbs were used as food by many Indigenous peoples and settlers. Large meadows containing the plants were closely guarded.

Marsh Skullcap

Scutellaria galericulata

MINT FAMILY

This plant grows to 80 cm tall at low to mid-elevations in wetlands, along lakeshores and stream banks and in ditches. Its leaves are opposite, oval to lance-shaped and irregularly scalloped along the blades. The stem is square, typical of the mint family. The trumpet-shaped flowers have a hooded upper lip and a broad, hairless lower lip, and are blue to purplish-pink marked with white. The flowers occur as solitary on slender stalks or as pairs in the leaf axils.

Dame's Rocket
(Dame's Violet)

Hesperis matronalis

MUSTARD FAMILY

This mustard was introduced into North America from Eurasia as an ornamental plant, and it has spread extensively throughout Canada and much of the United States. Typically it inhabits disturbed sites, waste ground, thickets, woods and road- and railsides. The plant is erect and grows to over 1 m tall. Its lance-shaped leaves are alternate, predominantly clasping on the stem, hairy on both sides, and become progressively smaller up the stem. The flowers occur in showy clusters at the top of the stem. Each flower is four-petalled, purple to blue to white in colour, and fragrant.

Bladder Locoweed
(Stalked Pod
Crazyweed)

Oxytropis podocarpa

PEA FAMILY

This alpine plant grows on gravelly slopes, high above timberline, from a stout taproot that produces a rosette of leaves that lies flat on the ground. The leaves are covered with silvery hairs, and consist of 11–23 short, linear leaflets. The flower stalks are leafless, and rise just above the leaves, terminating with two or three pale-purple, pea-like flowers about 2 cm long. Each flower has a dark-purple, hairy calyx, with a characteristic beaked keel formed from the two lower fused petals.

Silky Lupine

Lupinus sericeus

PEA FAMILY

This is a leafy, erect, tufted perennial with stout stems that appears in sandy to gravelly grasslands, open woods, and roadsides, often growing in dense clumps or bunches. The plant grows up to 80 cm tall. The flowers are showy in long, dense terminal clusters, and display a variety of colours in blues and purples, occasionally white and yellow. The flowers have a typical pea shape, with a strongly truncated keel and a pointed tip. The leaves of Lupines are very distinctive, being palmately compound and alternate on the stem, with five to nine very narrow leaflets that have silky hairs on both sides.

Jacob's Ladder (Showy Jacob's Ladder)

Polemonium pulcherrimum

PHLOX FAMILY

This plant grows in dry, open, rocky environments in the montane to alpine zones. The leaves are distinctive, being pinnately compound, with 11–25 leaflets that are evenly spaced, resembling a tiny ladder. The leaf arrangement gives the plant its common name, a reference to the story in the Book of Genesis of how Jacob found a ladder to heaven. The pale- to dark-blue, cup-shaped flowers appear in an open cluster at the top of the stem and have a vivid orange ring at the base of the cup. The plant has a foul odour.

Shooting Star
Dodecatheon pulchellum

PRIMROSE FAMILY

This plant is scattered and locally common at low to alpine elevations in warm, dry climates, grasslands, mountain meadows and stream banks. The leaves are lance- to spatula-shaped and appear in a basal rosette. The singular to several purple to lavender flowers nod atop a leafless stalk, with corolla lobes turned backwards. The stamens are united into a yellow to orange tube from which the style and anthers protrude. A harbinger of spring, these lovely flowers often bloom in huge numbers, turning the grasslands to a purple hue.

Marsh Cinquefoil
Potentilla palustris

ROSE FAMILY

This plant inhabits bogs, marshes, streams and ponds from valleys to the subalpine zone. It grows from long, smooth rhizomes, creeping along the ground and rooting at the nodes. The leaves are usually smooth and pinnately compound, with five to seven obovate (teardrop-shaped) leaflets that are deeply toothed. While other members of the *Potentilla* family have yellow or white to cream-coloured flowers, Marsh Cinquefoil has purple to deep-red flowers. The flowers have an offensive, rotten odour that attracts insects as pollinators.

Purple Saxifrage (Purple Mountain Saxifrage)

Saxifraga oppositifolia

SAXIFRAGE FAMILY

This plant is a very low, matted, cushion-forming plant with tightly packed stems, common to rocky talus slopes, ledges and boulder fields in the alpine zone, particularly on calcium-rich substrates. The five-petalled purple to pink flowers appear singly on short stems. The opposite, stalkless leaves appear whorled. Each leaf is broadly wedge-shaped and bluish-green. Purple Saxifrage is the official flower of Nunavut.

Early Blue Violet (Western Long-Spurred Violet)

Viola adunca

VIOLET FAMILY

A plant of grasslands, open woods and slopes, this violet is widespread in North America and is highly variable. The flower colour ranges from blue to purple, and the three lower petals are often whitish at the base, pencilled with darker-purple guidelines. The largest petal has a hooked spur half as long as the lower petal. The mostly basal leaves are oval with a heart-shaped base and have round teeth on the margins. The plant grows low to the ground.

Silky Phacelia
(Silky Scorpionweed)

Phacelia sericea

WATERLEAF FAMILY

This spectacular plant grows on dry, rocky, open slopes at moderate to high elevations. The leaves are deeply divided into many segments and covered with silky hairs. The purple to blue flowers occur in clusters up a spike, resembling a bottle brush. The individual flowers are funnel-shaped, with long, purple, yellow-tipped stamens sticking out. The clusters of coiled branches resemble scorpion tails, thus the common name. The flowers of this plant are quite stunning, and having once seen them, one is unlikely to forget it.

Thread-Leaved
Phacelia
(Thread-Leaved
Scorpionweed)

Phacelia linearis

WATERLEAF FAMILY

This annual species of *Phacelia* occurs in the southern part of the region, but is more common east of the coastal mountains. It grows to 50 cm tall, and appears on dry plateaus and foothills. Its hairy, alternate leaves are thin and linear below, developing side lobes higher on the stem. The lavender to blue flowers are reasonably large and appear in open clusters from the leaf axils.

Red, Orange *and* Pink Flowers

This section contains flowers that are red, orange or pink when encountered in the field. Flowers that are pinkish often can have tones running to lavender, so if you do not find the flower you are looking for here, check the other sections of the book.

Falsebox

Paxistima myrsinites

BITTERSWEET FAMILY

This dense evergreen shrub grows at low to mid-elevations in coniferous forests. Its reddish-brown branches exhibit four ridges, and its glossy, leathery leaves are opposite and sharp-toothed. The tiny, fragrant flowers are relatively inconspicuous, being brick-red to maroon and cruciform, with four petals occurring in clusters along the branches in the leaf axils. The plant is also known as Mountain Boxwood, Oregon Boxwood and Mountain-Lover.

Mountain Sorrel

Oxyria digyna

BUCKWHEAT FAMILY

This relatively low-growing plant often appears in clumps along streams, at lake margins and in moist rocky places in the subalpine and alpine zones. Its long-stalked, primarily basal, often reddish leaves are smooth with wavy margins and distinctively kidney- or heart-shaped. The tiny green to reddish flowers appear in crowded clusters along several upright stems and are relatively inconspicuous. The fruits are flat, red, papery seeds that have broad translucent wings. Mammals and birds eat this species, and a number of Indigenous peoples also used it as a food.

Water Smartweed (Water Knotweed)

Polygonum amphibium

BUCKWHEAT FAMILY

This plant occurs from prairie to subalpine elevations, and is found in ponds, marshes and ditches and along lakeshores, often forming mats in standing water. The plant may grow on land adjacent to or in water. The leaves are large, oblong to lance-shaped, rounded or pointed at the tips, and have a prominent mid-vein. The flowers are pink and occur in a dense, oblong cluster at the top of thick, smooth stalks. The plant was used by Indigenous peoples both medicinally in poultices to treat piles and skin disease, and as a food. The plant is also food for a large variety of birds.

Red Columbine (Western Columbine)

Aquilegia formosa

BUTTERCUP FAMILY

These beautiful flowers are found in meadows and dry to moist woods, and are among the showiest of all the western wildflowers. The leaves of the plant are mostly basal and compound, with three sets of three leaflets each. The flowers occur on stems above the basal leaves, and are composed of five yellow petal blades and five red sepals with straight spurs at their ends. The leaves on the flowering stem are considerably smaller than the basal leaves, appearing with only three leaflets each. Numerous stamens extend well beyond the petals.

Western Meadow Rue

Thalictrum occidentale

BUTTERCUP FAMILY

This plant is a dioecious species, meaning that the male and female flowers are found on separate plants. The leaves are very similar in appearance to those of Columbines (*Aquilegia*), occurring in threes, but this plant's leaves are three times ternate – 3 × 3 × 3 – for a total of 27 leaflets per leaf. Neither gender of flowers has any petals. The male flower resembles a small wind chime, with the stamens hanging down like tassels. The female flowers resemble small, star-shaped pinwheels. The plant prefers cool, moist forest environments. Indigenous peoples used the species variously as a medicine, a love charm, and a stimulant for horses.

Windflower

Anemone multifida

BUTTERCUP FAMILY

This plant favours south-facing slopes, grasslands and open woods. Like all anemones, Windflowers possess no petals, only sepals. The flowers are a variety of colours, from white to yellowish to red, and appear atop a woolly stem. Beneath the flowers are bract-like leaves attached directly to the stem. The leaves are palmate, with deeply incised, silky-haired leaflets, somewhat reminiscent of poppy leaves. The fruits are achenes in a rounded head, which later form a large, cottony mass. The common name, Windflower, comes from the method of distributing the long-plumed seeds of the plant.

Common Burdock
Arctium minus

COMPOSITE FAMILY

A plant of pastures, roadsides, fencerows and disturbed sites, Common Burdock is erect with spreading branches and grows to over 1 m tall. The flowers appear at the ends of the branches as purplish to pinkish tubular protrusions with disc florets only. The outer bracts are decidedly hooked at the ends, and form a ball around the inflorescence, making the plant appear to be furry and unkempt. These hooks are extraordinarily efficient in disseminating the seeds of the plant, clinging as they do to fur on animals and clothing on humans who encounter the plant in the field.

Orange Hawkweed
Hieracium aurantiacum

COMPOSITE FAMILY

Common to open woods, meadows, roadsides, ditches and disturbed areas from low to subalpine areas, this conspicuous flower was introduced from Europe, where it has long been a garden ornamental. The species can spread rapidly and become a noxious weed. The orange flower heads appear in a cluster on ascending stalks. The flowers are composed entirely of ray florets; there are no disc florets. The leaves are broadly lance- to spoon-shaped, in a basal rosette. The reference to hawk in the name arises from an ancient belief that eating these plants improved a hawk's vision.

Black Gooseberry (Swamp Currant)

Ribes lacustre

CURRANT FAMILY

This erect deciduous shrub grows up to 150 cm tall in moist woods and open areas from foothills to the subalpine zone. The branches of the plant have small prickles and stout thorns at leaf and branch bases. The leaves are alternate and shaped like maple leaves, with three to five deeply cleft, palmate lobes. The reddish, saucer-shaped flowers hang in elongated clusters. The fruits are dark-purple to black berries that bristle with tiny hairs. The genus *Ribes* includes all Currants and Gooseberries. Gooseberries are bristly hairy, while Currants are not.

Flowering Red Currant (Red-Flower Currant)

Ribes sanguineum

CURRANT FAMILY

This early-blooming plant is an upright shrub that grows to 3 m tall in open, dry woods, along roadsides and in logged areas from low to mid-elevations. It has reddish-brown bark, and its triangular leaves are deeply three-lobed, toothed and up to 6 cm wide. The numerous flowers are rose-red to pink, tubular with five spreading lobes, and occur in clusters of 10–20 flowers blooming together. The round, black fruits are often covered with a blue bloom and are unpalatable.

Spreading Dogbane

Apocynum androsaemifolium

DOGBANE FAMILY

This relatively common shrub occurs in thickets and wooded areas, and has freely branching, slender stems. The egg-shaped leaves are opposite and have sharp-pointed tips. The small, white to light-pinkish, bell-shaped flowers droop from the ends of the leafy stems, usually in clusters. The petal lobes are spreading and bent back, usually with dark-pink veins. Indigenous peoples used the tough fibres from these plants to fashion strong thread for making items like bowstrings and fishing nets. The pods of the plant are poisonous if eaten.

Fireweed (Great Willowherb)

Chamaenerion angustifolium (form. *Epilobium angustifolium*)

EVENING PRIMROSE FAMILY

This plant occurs along roadsides and in disturbed areas, clearings and shaded woods from low elevations to the subalpine. It is often one of the first plants to appear after a fire. The pink, four-petalled flowers bloom in long terminal clusters. Bracts between the petals are narrow. The flowers bloom from the bottom of the cluster first, then upward on the stem. The leaves are alternate and appear whorled. Fireweed is the floral emblem of the Yukon.

River Beauty (Broad-Leaved Willowherb)

Chamaenerion latifolium (form. *Epilobium latifolium*)

EVENING PRIMROSE FAMILY

This plant grows as a pioneer, often in dense colonies, on gravelly floodplains and river bars, where its dense leaves and waving pink to purple flowers often obscure the stony ground underneath. River Beauty strongly resembles common Fireweed in appearance, but it has much shorter stems, broader leaves and larger, more brilliantly coloured flowers. The flowers bloom in a loose, short, leafy inflorescence. The leaves are bluish-green and waxy, with rounded tips. The plant is also known as Dwarf Fireweed.

Elephant's Head

Pedicularis groenlandica

FIGWORT FAMILY

This is a plant of wet meadows, stream banks and wetland margins. Its flowers appear in dense clusters atop a substantial stalk that can grow to 50 cm tall. Each of the flowers is reddish-purple to pinkish, and has an uncanny resemblance to an elephant's head, with a curved trunk and flared ears.

All members of this genus are somewhat parasitic on the roots of other plants, so transplantation is doomed to failure. When encountered, a close examination of this delightful flower is recommended, but be careful of the fragile habitat in which it lives.

Red Monkeyflower (Lewis's Monkeyflower)

Mimulus lewisii

FIGWORT FAMILY

This plant occurs, often in large patches, along mountain streams and in other moist areas in the sub-alpine and alpine zones. The clasping, conspicuously veined leaves are opposite and have irregular teeth along their margins. The showy red flowers arise from the axils of the upper leaves. The flowers are funnel-shaped, with two lips which are hairy and have yellow markings. Hummingbirds and bees are attracted to these flowers.

Red Paintbrush

Castilleja miniata

FIGWORT FAMILY

A plant of alpine meadows, well-drained slopes, open subalpine forests, moist stream banks and open foothills woods, Paintbrush is widely distributed and extremely variable in colour. Its narrow, sharp-pointed leaves are linear to lance-shaped and usually without teeth or divisions, though sometimes the upper leaves have three shallow lobes. The showy red, leafy bracts, which are actually modified leaves, resemble a brush dipped in paint, hence the common name.

Thin-Leaved Owl's Clover

Orthocarpus tenuifolius

FIGWORT FAMILY

This plant grows up to 30 cm tall at low to subalpine elevations in dry grasslands and forests. Its leaves are alternate, linear, unstalked and up to 5 cm long. The inflorescence is a dense, prominently bracted terminal spike. The petal-like bracts are broad, blunt tipped and pinkish-purple in colour. Owl's Clovers are very similar to the Paintbrushes (*Castillejas*), but the latter are mostly perennial, while the Owl's Clovers are annuals.

Bog Cranberry

Vaccinium oxycoccos
(also *Oxycoccus oxycoccos*)

HEATH FAMILY

This plant is a creeping, vine-like dwarf evergreen shrub that grows up to 40 cm tall in bogs and in wet sphagnum moss from low to sub-alpine elevations. Its stems are thin, wiry and slightly hairy. The small leaves are alternate, leathery, sharp-pointed and widely spaced on the stem. The leaves are dark green on the upper surface, lighter underneath, and the margins curl under. The nodding flowers are deep pink, with four petals that curve backwards.

False Azalea (Fool's Huckleberry)

Menziesia ferruginea (also *Rhododendron menziesii*)

HEATH FAMILY

This deciduous shrub is erect and spreading, and grows up to 2 m tall in moist, wooded sites from foot-hills to subalpine zones. The twigs of the shrub have fine, rust-col-oured, sticky glandular hairs, and give off a skunky odour when crushed. The leaves are alternate, elliptical and glandular hairy, with a prominent mid-vein. The small, greenish-orange to pink-ish flowers are urn-shaped and nodding on long, slender stalks. The fruits are dark-purplish capsules which are inedible.

Pine-Drops

Pterospora andromedea

HEATH FAMILY

Pine-Drops is a rare saprophyte, a plant that gets its nutrients from decaying plant or animal matter. It grows to 1 m tall in deep humus of coniferous or mixed woods. Its leaves are mostly basal and resemble scales. The flowers are cream-coloured to yellowish, and occur in a raceme that covers roughly the top half of the stalk. The petals are united into an urn shape, and hang downward off bent flower stalks, like small lanterns. The stalks of the plant will remain erect for a year or more after the plant dies.

Pink Wintergreen

Pyrola asarifolia

HEATH FAMILY

This plant is an erect perennial that inhabits moist to dry coniferous and mixed forests and riverine environments from the montane to the subalpine zone. Its waxy, pale-pink to purplish-red nodding flowers are shaped like an inverted cup or bell and have a long, curved, projecting style. The shiny, rounded, dark-green leaves are basal in a rosette and have a leathery appearance. The name "wintergreen" refers to this plant's evergreen leaves, not the flavour that has the same name.

Pipsissewa (Prince's-Pine)

Chimaphila umbellata

HEATH FAMILY

This small evergreen shrub grows to 30 cm tall in coniferous woods. Its glossy, dark-green leaves are narrowly spoon-shaped and saw-toothed, and occur in whorls. The waxy pink flowers are saucer-shaped and nodding on an erect stem above the leaves. The fruits of the plant are dry, round, brown capsules that often overwinter on the stem. "Pipsissewa" is an adaptation of the Cree name for the plant.

Red Heather (Pink Mountain Heather)

Phyllodoce empetriformis

HEATH FAMILY

This dwarf evergreen shrub grows up to 30 cm tall, and thrives in sub-alpine and alpine meadows and on slopes near timberline. Its blunt, needle-like leaves are grooved on both sides. The red to pink, urn-shaped flowers are erect and/or nodding in clusters at the top of the stems. This plant is not a true heather, but it has been called by that name for so long that it might as well be.

Swamp Laurel (Western Bog Laurel)

Kalmia microphylla

HEATH FAMILY

This low-growing evergreen shrub occurs in cool bogs and along stream banks and lakeshores from low to sub-alpine elevations. Its leathery leaves are dark green above and greyish-white beneath, often with the margins rolled under. The flowers are pink to rose coloured, with the petals fused together to form a saucer or bowl on a reddish stalk. There are 10 purple-tipped stamens protruding from the petals. The leaves and flowers of this plant contain poisonous alkaloids that can be fatal to humans and livestock if ingested.

Orange Honeysuckle (Western Trumpet)

Lonicera ciliosa

HONEYSUCKLE FAMILY

This is a climbing vine up to 6 m long that clambers over trees and shrubs in woodlands and forest openings from low to high elevations. Its broadly elliptical leaves are up to 10 cm long and opposite on the stem, except the uppermost pair, which are connate – fused at their bases to form a shallow cup. The vividly orange, tubular flowers are up to 4 cm long and appear in clusters of up to 25 blooms from inside the connate leaves. Unlike many members of the genus, these flowers have no scent.

Twinflower

Linnaea borealis

HONEYSUCKLE FAMILY

This small, trailing evergreen is common in coniferous forests, but is easily overlooked by the casual observer. The plant sends runners creeping along the forest floor, over mosses, stumps and fallen logs. At frequent intervals the runners give rise to the distinctive Y-shaped stems 5–10 cm tall. Each fork of the stem supports at its end a pink to white, slightly flared, trumpet-like flower that hangs down like a small lantern on a tiny lamppost. The flowers have a sweet perfume that is most evident near evening.

Tiger Lily (Columbia Lily)

Lilium columbianum

LILY FAMILY

This showy lily can have up to 30 flowers per stem. The orange to orange-yellow blossoms hang downward, with reflexed petals, and have deep-red to purplish spots near the base. These spots are most probably the source of the common name Tiger Lily. The bulbs of the plants were used as food by some Indigenous peoples. They were said to have a peppery taste and would add that flavour to other foods. Over-picking has diminished the distribution of the plant.

Nodding Onion

Allium cernuum

LILY FAMILY

This plant is a common species in the region, and is easily identified by its smooth, leafless stem and drooping or nodding pink inflorescence. There are usually 8–12 flowers in the nodding cluster. The stem gives off a strong oniony odour when crushed. Indigenous peoples consumed the bulbs, both raw and cooked and as flavouring for other foods, and dried them for later use.

Sagebrush Mariposa Lily

Calochortus macrocarpus

LILY FAMILY

This is a large lily that occurs in the region in dry grasslands and open ponderosa forests. It has pinkish to purplish hues on the petals, which are decidedly pointed, and display a crescent-shaped gland at the base of each one. This plant grows in more arid environments and blooms later than does the Three Spot Mariposa Lily (*C. apiculatus*). The range of this plant has been severely restricted over the years by cattle grazing. The plant will not accept transplantation, so it is best to enjoy it in the wild where it grows.

Western Wood Lily
Lilium philadelphicum

LILY FAMILY

This lily grows in moist meadows and dense to open woods and at the edges of aspen groves from prairie elevations to the low subalpine zone. Its leaves are numerous, lance-shaped, smooth and alternate on the stem, except for the upper leaves, which are in whorls. Each plant may produce from one to five bright-orange to orange-red flowers, each with three virtually identical sepals and petals. This plant is often confused with the Columbia Lily (*L. columbianum*), which is coloured similarly, but the tepals on the Columbia Lily are reflexed, while the petals on the Wood Lily are held in a chalice shape.

Mountain Hollyhock
Iliamna rivularis

MALLOW FAMILY

This large plant can grow up to 2 m tall, and appears in montane to subalpine elevations on moist slopes and stream banks and in meadows. The leaves are fairly large, alternate and irregularly toothed, resembling maple leaves, with five to seven lobes each. The relatively large, pink to whitish, saucer-shaped flowers resemble garden Hollyhocks. They appear from the leaf axils along the stem and at the tips of the stems, in long, interrupted clusters. The flowers have many stamens, the filaments of which are united at the base to form a tube.

Showy Milkweed

Asclepias speciosa

MILKWEED FAMILY

This perennial plant is rather spectacular with its tall, coarse stem, large leaves and round clusters of pink to purple flowers. It grows up to 2 m tall from a thick, creeping rootstock, often occurring in clumps. It is found in thickets and moist grasslands and along roadsides and streams. Its thick, dark-green leaves are opposite, short-stalked, oblong or oval, prominently veined, and rounded at the tip, sometimes having a sharp spine. The flowers have a strong scent and occur in dense, rounded, umbrella-shaped clusters that can span 7 cm across.

Wild Bergamot

Monarda fistulosa

MINT FAMILY

This showy flower inhabits grasslands and open woods, blooming in the summer months. The stems of the plant are erect and square, with a strong and distinctive odour of mint. The stem is topped with a dense cluster of pink to violet flowers. The leaves are opposite, triangular to ovate in shape and pointed at the ends. Some Indigenous peoples used the plant as a perfume, meat preservative and insect repellent. It is also reported that the plant was used ceremonially in the Sun Dance.

Venus Slipper
(Fairy Slipper)

Calypso bulbosa

ORCHID FAMILY

This orchid is found in moist, shaded coniferous forests. Its flowers are solitary and nodding on leafless stems. The flower has pinkish to purplish sepals and mauve side petals. The lip is whitish or purplish with red to purple spots or stripes and is hairy yellow inside. The flower is on the top of a single stalk and has a deeply wrinkled appearance. This small but extraordinarily beautiful flower blooms in the early spring, often occurring in colonies.

Spotted Coralroot
(Summer Coralroot)

Corallorhiza maculata

ORCHID FAMILY

A plant of moist woods and bogs, this orchid grows from extensive coral-like rhizomes. There are no leaves, but the plant has several membranous bracts that sheath the purplish to brownish stem. A number of flowers appear on each stem, loosely arranged up the stem in a raceme. The three sepals and two upper petals are reddish purple. The lip petal is white with dark-red or purple spots and two lateral lobes. The plant lacks chlorophyll and does not produce food by photosynthesis, relying instead on parasitizing fungi in the soil.

Scarlet Gilia (Skyrocket)

Ipomopsis aggregata

PHLOX FAMILY

This plant is a biennial that occurs in semi-desert areas, on open rocky slopes and in dry meadows, grasslands and open forests at low to moderately high elevations. In the first year, the plant puts out a rosette of basal leaves that are arranged pinnately into numerous narrow segments. The leaves emit a skunk-like odour when crushed. In the second year, the plant puts up one to several flowering stems to 1 m tall which are sticky-hairy on the upper parts. The numerous flowers are clustered at the tops of the stems. The flowers are fiery red and trumpet-shaped.

Bitterroot

Lewisia rediviva

PURSLANE FAMILY

This is a plant of rocky slopes, dry grasslands and sagebrush slopes of the inter-mountain region. Its strikingly beautiful flowers are deep pink to sometimes white and have about 15 narrow petals. The flowers occur on such short stalks that they virtually appear to rest on the soil's surface. The flowers only open in the sun. The leaves are all basal, appearing in the spring but withering and receding into the ground prior to the flower blooming. The Bitterroot was used as food and as a trading item by many Indigenous peoples.

Hardhack (Douglas Spirea)

Spiraea douglasii

ROSE FAMILY

This erect, deciduous, freely branching shrub forms dense, impenetrable thickets up to 2 m tall in marshy areas and along streams at low to mid-elevations. The leaves are oblong, elliptical, 3–9 cm long and notched at the tips. The inflorescence is a tall, elongated cluster of hundreds of tiny pink flowers. The flowers are relatively short-lived, quickly turning brown and drab in appearance.

The common name, Hardhack, is said to arise because the dense thickets of the plant are hard to hack through.

Three-Flowered Avens (Old Man's Whiskers)

Geum triflorum

ROSE FAMILY

This plant is widespread in arid basins and on dry plateaus and open grasslands from prairies to subalpine elevations. Its hairy, dull purplish to pinkish flowers bloom in early spring, nodding at the top of the stem, usually in clusters of three though some plants can have as many as five on a single stem. The flowers remain semi-closed and do not open completely the way many common flowers do. The fruits are feathery clusters of brownish to purplish, plume-like achenes (small, dry, one-seeded fruits) that are sown by wind action. Indeed, when these seeds were being blown by the wind, many early settlers referred to the phenomenon as "prairie smoke," accounting for another common name for the species.

Prickly Rose
Rosa acicularis

ROSE FAMILY

This is a deciduous shrub that grows up to 150 cm tall, with freely branched stems, and thorns at the base of each leaf. The flowers are pink with five broad petals. Leaves are oblong, notched and somewhat hairy below. The Prickly Rose will easily hybridize with other members of the rose family, and the hybrids can be difficult to identify specifically. The dark-red fruits are fleshy, round to oval hips with sepals remaining on top, like a beard. They are rich in vitamin C, and can be used to make a delicious jelly.

Roseroot
Rhodiola integrifolia (form. *Sedum integrifolium*)

STONECROP FAMILY

This plant occurs in the subalpine and alpine zones, favouring moist, rocky scree, talus and ridges. The stems arise from a fleshy rootstock, and they are covered in persistent leaves. The leaves are oval to oblong, fleshy and somewhat flattened. The rose-coloured to purple flowers have oblong petals and occur in dense, rounded, flat-topped clusters atop the stems. When the roots are cut or bruised, they give off the fragrance of roses, thus the common name.

White, Green *and* Brown Flowers

This section includes flowers that are predominantly white or cream-coloured, green or brown when encountered in the field. Given that some flowers fade to other colours as they age, if you do not find the one you are looking for here, check the other parts of the book.

Cushion Buckwheat (Silver-Plant)

Eriogonum ovalifolium

BUCKWHEAT FAMILY

This mat-forming species can be found from prairie elevations to the alpine ridges. Its large mats are distinctive and appealing to the eye on high rocky ridges. The leaves are oval in shape and densely covered in silver woolly hairs, giving the plant an overall grey or silver ap-pearance. The white to cream-coloured flowers occur in dense, rounded heads atop short, leafless stems that rise from the basal growth. The flower umbels in this species are simple, not compound as in most members of the genus.

Sulphur Buckwheat

Eriogonum umbellatum

BUCKWHEAT FAMILY

This perennial grows from a stout taproot and tends to form mats. Its spoon- to egg-shaped leaves are all basal, narrowing to a slender stalk, greenish above and often woolly white beneath. The leaves turn bright red in the fall. The flowering stem is usually leafless and up to 30 cm tall. The stem supports an in-florescence composed of small creamy-white to pale-yellow flowers that are held in compact spherical clusters (umbels). The flowers sometimes become tinged with pink on aging. The plant occurs from moderate to alpine elevations, on grassy slopes, dry gravel ridges, alpine ridges and talus slopes.

The specific epithet, *umbellatum*, refers to the shape of the inflorescence, and in-deed the species also goes by the locally common name Subalpine Umbrellaplant.

Baneberry

Actaea rubra

BUTTERCUP FAMILY

This perennial grows up to 1 m tall in moist, shady woods and thickets, along streams and in clearings from low to subalpine elevations. The plant has one to several stout, upright, branching stems. Its coarse-toothed leaves are all on the stem and are divided two or three times into threes. The inflorescence is a dense, white, cone-shaped cluster of flowers that appears on top of a spike. The fruit is a large cluster of either shiny red or white berries. The leaves, roots and berries of this plant are extremely poisonous.

Globeflower

Trollius albiflorus

BUTTERCUP FAMILY

This plant grows from thick, fibrous rootstock in moist meadows, along stream banks and in open, damp areas in the subalpine and alpine zones. Its shiny, bright green, mostly basal leaves are palmately divided into five to seven parts and deeply toothed. The few stem leaves are alternate and short-stalked. The flowers are made up of five to ten white sepals (which may have a pinkish tint on the outside) that surround a central core filled with numerous dark-yellow stamens. This plant contains a poisonous alkaloid.

Mountain Marsh Marigold

Caltha leptosepala

BUTTERCUP FAMILY

This plant lives along stream banks and in marshes and seeps in the subalpine and alpine zones. Its simple, long-stemmed, mostly basal leaves are oblong to blunt-arrowhead-shaped, with wavy or round-toothed margins. The flowers are solitary on the end of the stem, and consist of up to a dozen white, petal-like sepals that are tinged with blue on the back. The flower has a bright-yellow centre composed of numerous stamens and pistils. This plant contains glucosides which are poisonous.

Water Crowfoot (Water Buttercup)

Ranunculus aquatilis

BUTTERCUP FAMILY

This aquatic Buttercup lives in ponds, lakes, ditches and slow-moving streams. Its white flowers have five sepals, five to ten petals and numerous pistils and stamens. The plant has two types of leaves. The submerged leaves are matting, thread-like filaments, while the floating leaves are deeply cleft into three to five lobes. The flowers are flecked with gold at the base, and are buoyed above the water on short stems. Yellow Water Crowfoot, which has yellow petals, is now considered to be in the same species.

Western Anemone (Chalice Flower)

Pulsatilla occidentalis (also *Anemone occidentalis*)

BUTTERCUP FAMILY

This plant is considered by many to be emblematic of wet alpine meadows and clearings. Its large, creamy-white flowers bloom early in the spring as the leaves are beginning to emerge. The entire plant is covered with hairs, which keep it protected in its cold habitat. Most of the leaves are basal, but there is a ring of feathery, grey-green stem leaves just below the flower. The flower is replaced by a clump of plumed seeds at the tip of the flowering stem. Some people refer to this stage as "Hippies on a Stick."

Western Clematis (White Virgin's Bower)

Clematis ligusticifolia

BUTTERCUP FAMILY

This plant is a climbing or trailing woody vine that occurs in coulees, creek bottoms and river valleys. It clings to and climbs over other plants by a twist or kink in its leaf stalks. Its leaves are opposite and compound, with five to seven long-stalked leaflets. The flowers are white and borne in dense clusters. The flowers are unisexual. The male flowers have many stamens, but no pistils, while the female ones have both pistils and sterile stamens.

Cow Parsnip

Heracleum lanatum

CARROT FAMILY

A denizen of shaded riverine habitat, stream banks, seeps and moist open woods, this plant grows to more than 2 m tall. The flowers are distinctive in large, compound, umbrella-shaped clusters (umbels) composed of numerous white flowers, with petals in fives. The leaves, compound in threes, are usually very large, softly hairy, toothed and deeply-lobed.

Large-Fruited Desert-Parsley

Lomatium macrocarpum

CARROT FAMILY

This stout, low-lying perennial grows from an elongated taproot and puts up a stem that branches near the base and grows up to 50 cm tall in dry or gravelly areas and on open slopes. The leaves are all basal, hairy, greyish in colour and finely dissected, resembling fern leaves. The white to purplish flowers occur in large umbrella-shaped clusters at the top of the multiple stems. The fruits are long and smooth, with narrow wings.

Sharptooth Angelica (Lyall's Angelica)

Angelica arguta

CARROT FAMILY

This plant can grow to over 2 m tall in shaded riverine habitat and moist open woods. The numerous white flowers are arranged in compound umbels. The leaves are twice compound, with large, sharp-toothed leaflets, as is reflected in the common name. The lateral leaf veins are directed to the ends of the teeth on the leaf margin. Angelicas are highly prized by herbalists for treating digestive disorders.

Water Hemlock

Cicuta maculata
(also *C. douglasii*)

CARROT FAMILY

This is a plant of marshes, river and stream banks, and low, wet areas. It produces several large umbrella-like clusters (compound umbels) of white flowers appearing at the top of a sturdy stalk. The leaves are alternate and twice compound, with many lance-shaped leaflets. The primary lateral veins in the leaves end between the notched teeth on the leaflets rather than at their points. This is unique, and separates this species from parsley family members in the area.

While lovely to look at, the Water Hemlock is considered to be perhaps the most poisonous plant in North America. All parts of the plant are toxic, as testified to by several of its common names, including Children's Bane, Beaver Poison and Death Of Man.

Hooker's Thistle

Cirsium hookerianum

COMPOSITE FAMILY

This native thistle can grow up to 1 m tall, and is found in a variety of habitats from valleys up to alpine elevations. The flower heads are white, and the bracts surrounding the flowers point upward. The leaves, stems and bracts are all covered with silky hairs. The leaves display a prominent mid-vein. The species name celebrates Sir William Hooker, a prestigious English botanist. This plant was used as food by some Indigenous peoples, eaten either raw or cooked.

Palmate Coltsfoot
Petasites frigidus

COMPOSITE FAMILY

This perennial grows from a thick, creeping rhizome, putting up a white-hairy flowering stem that is up to 50 cm tall in wet to moist forests and wetlands and along streams, rivers and lakeshores. The stem appears before the leaves do. The hairy, long-stalked basal leaves are kidney-shaped to round and palmately lobed. The stem leaves are very much reduced to reddish bracts. The inflorescence occurs as a flat-topped cluster of composite heads at the top of the stem. The flower heads have white to pinkish ray and disc florets or may appear with disc florets only. The flower heads have woolly-hairy bases.

Pathfinder Plant (Trail Plant)
Adenocaulon bicolor

COMPOSITE FAMILY

This species grows in shady and open woods at low to moderate elevations. Its somewhat large basal leaves are triangular, alternate and narrowly scalloped, and can reach 1 m long. The leaves are green above and white woolly beneath. The flowering stem is solitary with many branches, rising above the leaves, and has inconspicuous white flowers at the top. The fruits are hooked achenes that cling to clothing or fur of passersby. The common name arises because the leaves invert when a hiker passes through, leaving a trail of silvery-white undersides apparent.

Yarrow

Achillea millefolium

COMPOSITE FAMILY

This is a plant of dry to moist grasslands, open riverine forests, aspen woods and disturbed areas. The individual white flower heads appear in a dense, flat-topped or rounded terminal cluster. The ray florets are white to cream coloured (sometimes pink), and the central disc florets are straw coloured. The leaves are woolly, greyish to blue-green and finely divided, resembling a fern. Yarrow can occur in large colonies. The genus name, *Achillea*, is in honour of Achilles, the Greek warrior.

Northern Black Currant (Skunk Currant)

Ribes hudsonianum

CURRANT FAMILY

This plant is an erect deciduous shrub that grows up to 2 m tall in moist to wet forests at low to sub-alpine elevations. The species does not have thorns, but has yellow resin glands dotting its smooth bark. The leaves are alternate and maple-leaf-shaped, with three to five rounded lobes. The white, saucer-shaped flowers occur in spreading to erect clusters and have a strong smell that some people find uncomfortable. The black fruits are speckled with resin dots, and are said to have a particularly bitter taste.

Sticky Currant

Ribes viscosissimum

CURRANT FAMILY

This plant is a shrub that grows up to 2 m high in damp woods and clearings from valleys to subalpine elevations. It does not have prickles. Its bell-shaped flowers are yellowish-white, often tinged with pink. The flowers and leaves are covered in glandular hairs that are sticky to the touch. The blue-black fruits also are sticky and not considered edible. The specific epithet, *viscosissimum*, is the superlative form of the Latin *viscosus*, meaning "stickiest."

Bunchberry (Dwarf Dogwood)

Cornus canadensis

DOGWOOD FAMILY

This is a plant of moist coniferous woods, often found on rotting logs and stumps. The flowers are clusters of inconspicuous greenish-white flowers set among four white, petal-like showy bracts. The leaves are in a terminal whorl of four to seven, all prominently veined, and are dark green above, lighter underneath. The fruits are bright-red berries. The plant's common name, Bunchberry, is probably derived from the fact that the fruits are all bunched together in a terminal cluster when ripe.

Eyebright

Euphrasia nemorosa

FIGWORT FAMILY

These small, beautiful plants are found in moist woods at moderate to high elevations. They grow from a taproot that puts up slender, hairy, erect, sometimes branching stems that may reach 40 cm tall. The leaves are sessile (stalkless), egg-shaped to somewhat circular, sparsely hairy and glandular, and have decidedly toothed margins. The upper leaves are reduced in size, and the white flowers appear in the axils. The flowers are two-lipped, with the upper lip being bi-lobed and concave, the lower one having three spreading, notched lobes. There is purple pencilling on the lips and a yellow spot on the lower lip.

Sickletop Lousewort (Parrot's Beak)

Pedicularis racemosa

FIGWORT FAMILY

This lovely plant favours upper montane and subalpine environments. Its white flower has a very distinctive shape that deserves close examination to appreciate its intricacy. It is variously described as similar to a sickle, a tool with a short handle and a curved blade, or as resembling a parrot's beak, thus explaining the most often used common names. The flowers appear along a purplish stem that grows up to 35 cm tall. The simple leaves are lance-shaped to linear and have distinctive fine, sharp teeth on the margins. Another locally common name for this plant is Leafy Lousewort.

Beargrass

Xerophyllum tenax

LILY FAMILY

These impressive plants grow in peaty soil or clay in open woods and clearings from mid-elevations to the subalpine. The species has a basal clump of long, dense, sharp, evergreen leaves from which rises an impressive stem up to 150 cm tall. The inflorescence is a large torch-shaped cluster of hundreds of miniature white lilies which bloom from the bottom of the cluster first and then work their way upward. Individual plants may be sterile for several years, producing flowers only once to three times in a decade. Indigenous peoples used the leaves for weaving exquisite baskets, capes and hats.

Queen's Cup

Clintonia uniflora

LILY FAMILY

This beautiful perennial lily grows from slender rhizomes. Its flowers are about 5 cm in diameter, and are usually solitary, white and cup-shaped, appearing at the top of an erect, hairy stem. The plant may display two or three shiny leaves at the base of its flowering stem, each of them oblong or elliptical with hairy edges. Its fruit is a single deep-blue berry, giving rise to two locally common names: Beadlily and Bluebead Lily.

Three Spot Mariposa Lily (Three Spot Tulip)

Calochortus apiculatus

LILY FAMILY

This perennial lily inhabits coniferous woods; dry, sandy or gravelly slopes; and moist fescue grassland, from the montane to the subalpine zone. It grows from a bulb as a single-leafed plant producing one to five flowers. The flower is white to yellowish-white with three spreading petals fringed at the margins. Each petal is hairy on its inner surfaces and has a purplish gland at its base. These purple glands give the flower one of its common names, Three Spot Tulip. Three narrow white sepals appear between the petals.

Mariposa is Spanish for "butterfly."

Western Trillium (Western Wake Robin)

Trillium ovatum

LILY FAMILY

This gorgeous lily blooms early and prefers boggy, rich soils in montane and lower subalpine forests. Its large, distinctive, stalkless leaves are broadly egg-shaped with sharp tips, and occur in a whorl of three below the flower. The solitary flower blooms atop a short stem above the leaves, with three broad white petals up to 5 cm long alternating with three narrow green sepals. The petals change colour with age, first turning pink, then progressing to purple.

White Camas

Zigadenus elegans (also *Toxicoscordion elegans*)

LILY FAMILY

This plant of moist grasslands, grassy slopes and open woods grows from an onion-like bulb that has no oniony smell. The greenish-white, foul-smelling flowers appear in open clusters along an erect stem. There are yellowish-green v-shaped glands (nectaries) near the base of the petals and sepals. The leaves are mainly basal and resemble grass, with prominent mid-veins. The species name, *elegans*, means "elegant." Though elegant indeed, these plants are extremely poisonous, containing very toxic alkaloids, particularly in the bulbs.

Other common names include Mountain Death Camas, Green Lily, Elegant Poison Camas, Elegant Death Camas and Showy Death Camas

Reflexed Rock Cress

Arabis holboellii

MUSTARD FAMILY

This plant is widespread in the eastern parts of the region, especially on gravelly slopes and in dry open woods. The plant stands up to 70 cm tall. Its basal leaves form a rosette, and the stem leaves are numerous, narrow, lance-shaped, and clasping on the stem. The flowers are white to pinkish, occurring on reflexed stalks, hanging down along the stem and in a terminal cluster. Rock Cresses are edible and are said to have a taste similar to radishes. The leaves and flowers are often added to salads and sandwiches.

Heart-Leaved Twayblade

Listera cordata

ORCHID FAMILY

This small orchid, standing about 20 cm tall, prefers a cool, damp, mossy habitat. As a consequence of its size and preferred location, it is an easy flower to miss. Its white flowers are scattered up the stem in an open raceme. The lip of the flower is deeply split, almost in two. The stem leaf structure of the genus is distinctive, with two leaves appearing opposite each other partway up the stem. The specific epithet, *cordata*, means "heart-shaped," referring to the leaves.

Hooded Ladies' Tresses

Spiranthes romanzoffiana

ORCHID FAMILY

This orchid is reasonably common in swampy places, along lakeshores and in meadows and open, shady woods. It grows up to 60 cm tall. The characteristic feature of the plant is its crowded flower spike, which can contain up to 60 densely spaced white flowers that appear to coil around the end of the stem in three spiralling ranks. When newly bloomed, the flower has a wonderful aroma which most people say smells like vanilla. The common name is a reference to the braid-like appearance of the flowers, similar to a braid in a lady's hair.

Mountain Lady's Slipper

Cypripedium montanum

ORCHID FAMILY

This distinctive and relatively rare orchid grows up to 60 cm tall, occurring in dry to moist woods and open areas from mid- to subalpine elevations. Its lower petal forms a white, pouch-shaped lower lip that has purple markings. The brownish sepals and lateral petals have wavy margins and appear to spiral away from the stem. The attractive leaves are alternate, broadly elliptical and clasping on the stem and have prominent veins. One to three flowers can appear on the stem, and they are wonderfully fragrant.

Round-Leaved Orchid

Amerorchis rotundifolia

ORCHID FAMILY

This tiny orchid, standing no more than 25 cm tall, occurs in well-drained parts of bogs and swamps and in cool, moist, mossy coniferous forests. The flowers are irregular, with three white to pink sepals. The upper sepal combines with the upper two, purple-veined petals to form a hood. The two lateral sepals are wing-like. The lowest petal forms an oblong lip that is white to pink and spotted with dark-red or purple markings. The leaf is basal, solitary and broadly elliptical. These small orchids are always a treat to discover, and in some places they appear in profusion.

Sparrow's-Egg Lady's Slipper (Franklin's Lady's Slipper)

Cypripedium passerinum

ORCHID FAMILY

This lovely orchid grows from a cord-like rhizome along streams and in boggy places and mossy coniferous areas. It resembles other Lady's Slippers in shape, but this flower is decidedly smaller, with bright-purple dots on its interior, and has shorter, stubbier, greenish sepals. Both the stem and the leaves of the plant are covered in soft hairs. The specific epithet, *passerinum*, means "sparrow-like," a reference to the spotting on the flower being like the markings on a sparrow egg.

Wild Licorice

Glycyrrhiza lepidota

PEA FAMILY

This coarse perennial grows up to 1 m tall from a thick rootstock that has a slight licorice flavour and occurs in moist grasslands, along streams and rivers and in slough margins and disturbed areas. The leaves are alternate and pinnately compound, with 11–19 pale-green, sharp-pointed, lance-shaped leaflets. The leaflets have glandular dots on the underside and produce a lemony odour when crushed. The showy yellowish-white flowers are numerous and occur in dense clusters at the top of the stem.

Western Spring Beauty

Claytonia lanceolata

PURSLANE FAMILY

The flowers of this early bloomer are white, but may appear pink, owing to the reddish veins in the petals and the pink anthers. The tips of the petals are distinctly notched. The plants are usually less than 20 cm tall, and the flowers appear in loose, short-stalked terminal clusters. The species grows from a small, white, edible corm. Some Indigenous peoples used the corm as food, and it is said to taste similar to a potato.

Ocean Spray (Cream Bush)

Holodiscus discolor

ROSE FAMILY

This deciduous shrub is erect and loosely branched, growing to more than 3 m tall on coastal bluffs and in dry to moist woods. Its ovate leaves, toothed and lobed, are up to 8 cm long and woolly hairy underneath. The flowers are large pyramidal clusters of tiny white blooms that occur at the branch ends. The species is aptly named, as its clusters of white flowers bring to mind the foam cast up by crashing waves and ocean winds. The plant has a sweet scent from a distance, but is said to be musty smelling in close proximity.

Partridgefoot (Creeping Spiraea)

Luetkea pectinata

ROSE FAMILY

This dwarf evergreen shrub creates extensive mats as it creeps over the ground on scree slopes and in moist meadows and shady areas near timberline. It often grows where snow melts late in the season. Its numerous, mainly basal leaves are smooth, fan-shaped and much divided. Old leaves wither and persist for long periods of time. The white to cream-coloured flowers appear in short, crowded clusters atop erect stems. The flowers have four to six pistils and about 20 stamens, which are conspicuous on the flowers.

Alaska Saxifrage (Rusty Saxifrage)

Saxifraga ferruginea

SAXIFRAGE FAMILY

This plant grows in moist soils, on rocky outcrops and along spring banks in the subalpine and alpine zones. The stem at its base is unbranched and rust-coloured, which accounts for one of its common names. Its wedge- to spoon-shaped leaves are all basal in a rosette, with toothed margins and hairy stems. As the plant grows upward it begins to branch into multiple flowering stems. The five-petalled flowers bloom in an open inflorescence on hairy stems. The three upper petals are broader than the two lower ones. Each upper petal also has two yellow spots, while the lower ones have none. Some of the flowers will become leafy bulblets and drop off the plant.

Bishop's Cap (Bare-Stemmed Mitrewort)

Mitella nuda

SAXIFRAGE FAMILY

This wonderful species occurs along streams and in bogs, thickets and moist to dry forests from the montane to the subalpine. The plant stands erect and grows up to 20 cm tall. Its heart- to kidney-shaped leaves are basal and short-lobed, with rounded teeth. The tiny flowers occur in an open cluster scattered up the leafless stem. The saucer-shaped flowers are very distinctive, and when examined closely they are reminiscent of some kind of satellite dish such as might be found in outer space, complete with antennae festooned around the circumference of the flower.

Red-Stemmed Saxifrage

Saxifraga lyallii

SAXIFRAGE FAMILY

This plant occurs along stream banks and at seepages and other wet places in the high subalpine and alpine zones. It is often found growing in wet mosses at such elevations. The fan- to wedge-shaped leaves are basal, coarse-toothed and abruptly narrowing on long stalks. The flowering stems grow up to 30 cm tall, and each bears one to several tiny, white, star-shaped flowers on its upper parts. When mature the white petals are marked with greenish-yellow blotches, and the sepals are reflexed. The fruits are bright-red two- to four-pointed capsules.

Spotted Saxifrage
Saxifraga bronchialis

SAXIFRAGE FAMILY

These beautiful flowers inhabit rocky crevices, rock faces, screes and open slopes, often appearing as if by magic from the rocks. The white flowers appear in clusters at the top of the wiry brown stems, and have small red or yellow spots near the tips of the five petals. A close examination of this beautiful flower is well worth the time.

Woodland Star (Small-Flowered Woodland Star)
Lithophragma parviflorum

SAXIFRAGE FAMILY

This perennial grows up to 30 cm tall and occurs in low-elevation grasslands, open ponderosa pine stands and sagebrush areas. It blooms early in the spring. Its kidney-shaped leaves are mostly basal, with deeply cleft and divided blades. The flowers are white to pinkish and occur in clusters at the tip of the stem. The flowers are broadly funnel shaped, with five spreading, deeply lobed petals.

GLOSSARY

achene: A dry, single-seeded fruit that does not split open at maturity.

alternate: A reference to the arrangement of leaves on a stem where the leaves appear singly and staggered on opposite sides of the stem.

annual: A plant that completes its life cycle, from seed germination to production of new seed, within one year and then dies.

anther: The portion of the stamen (the male portion of a flower) that produces pollen.

axil: The upper angle formed where a leaf, branch or other organ is attached to a plant stem.

basal: A reference to leaves that occur at the bottom of the plant, usually near or on the ground.

berry: A fleshy, many-seeded fruit.

biennial: A plant that completes its life cycle in two years, normally producing leaves in the first year and flowers in the second, before dying.

blade: The body of a leaf, excluding the stalk.

bract: A reduced or otherwise modified leaf that is usually found near the flower of a plant but is not part of the flower. *See also* **florescence**; **inflorescence**.

bulb: An underground plant part derived from a short, often rounded shoot that is covered with scales or leaves.

calyx: The outer set of flower parts, usually composed of sepals.

capsule: A dry fruit with more than one compartment that splits open to release seeds.

clasping: In reference to a leaf that surrounds or partially wraps around a stem or branch.

composite inflorescence: A flower-like **inflorescence** of the Composite Family, made up of **ray flowers** and/or **disc flowers**. Where both ray and disc flowers exist, the ray flowers surround the disc flowers.

compound leaf: A leaf that is divided into two or many leaflets, each of which may look like a complete leaf but lacks buds. Compound leaves may have a variety of arrangements.

connate: In reference to leaves where two leaves are fused at their bases to form a shallow cup, often seen in the Honeysuckle Family.

corm: An enlarged base or stem resembling a bulb.

corolla: The collective term for the petals of the flower that are found inside the sepals.

cultivar: A cultivated variety of a wild plant.

cyme: A broad, flat-topped flower arrangement in which the inner, central flowers bloom first.

decumbent: In reference to a plant reclining, or lying on the ground with tip ascending.

disc flower: Any of the small tubular florets found in the central, clustered portion of the flower head of members of the Composite Family; also referred to as "disc florets."

dioecious: Having unisex flowers, where male and female flowers appear on separate plants. *See also* **monoecious**.

drupe: A fleshy or juicy fruit that covers a single, stony seed inside, e.g., a cherry or a peach.

drupelet: Any one part of an aggregate fruit (like a raspberry or blackberry), where each such part is a fleshy fruit that covers a single, stony seed inside.

elliptical: Ellipse-shaped, widest in the middle. *See also* **oval**.

elongate: Having a slender form, long in relation to width.

entire: In reference to a leaf edge that is smooth, without teeth or notches.

filament: The part of the stamen that supports the anther. Also can refer to any threadlike structure.

florescence: Generally the flowering part of a plant; the arrangement of the flowers on the stem; also referred to as **inflorescence**. *But see* **bract**.

floret: One of the small tubular flowers in the central, clustered portion of the flower head of members of the Composite Family; also known as **disc flower**.

follicle: A dry fruit composed of a single compartment that splits open along one side at maturity to release seeds.

fruit: The ripe ovary with the enclosed seeds, and any other structures that enclose it.

glabrous: In reference to a leaf surface, smooth, neither waxy or sticky.

gland: A small organ that secretes a sticky or oily substance and is attached to some part of the plant.

glaucous: Having a fine, waxy, often white coating that may be rubbed off; often characteristic of leaves, fruits and stems.

hood: in reference to flower structure, a curving or folded petal-like structure interior to the petals and exterior to the stamens in certain flowers.

host: In reference to a parasitic or semi-parasitic plant, the plant from which the parasite obtains its nourishment.

inflorescence: Generally the flowering part of a plant; the arrangement of the flowers on the stem; also referred to as **florescence**. *But see* **bract**.

keel: The two fused petals in flowers that are members of the Pea Family.

lance-shaped: In reference to leaf shape, much longer than wide, widest below the middle and tapering to the tip, like the blade of a lance.

leaflet: A distinct, leaflike segment of a compound leaf.

linear: Like a line; long, narrow and parallel-sided.

lobe: A reference to the arrangement of leaves, a segment of a divided plant part, typically rounded.

margin: The edge of a leaf or petal.

mat: A densely interwoven or tangled, low, ground-hugging growth.

midrib: The main rib of a leaf.

mid-vein : The middle vein of a leaf.

monoecious: A plant having unisex flowers, with separate male and female flowers on the same plant. *See also* **dioecious**.

nectary: A plant structure that produces and secretes nectar.

node: A joint on a stem or root.

noxious weed: A plant, usually imported, that out-competes and drives out native plants.

oblong: Somewhat rectangular, with rounded ends.

obovate: Shaped like a teardrop.

opposite: A reference to the arrangement of leaves on a stem where the leaves appear paired on opposite sides of the stem, directly across from each other.

oval: Broadly elliptical.

ovary: The portion of the flower where the seeds develop. It is usually a swollen area below the style and stigma.

ovate: Egg-shaped.

palmate: A reference to the arrangement of leaves on a stem where the leaves spread like the fingers on a hand, diverging from a central or common point.

panicle: A branched inflorescence that blooms from the bottom up.

pencilled: Marked with coloured lines, like the petals on Violets.

perennial: A plant that does not produce seeds or flowers until its second year of life, then lives for three or more years, usually flowering each year before dying.

petal: A component of the inner floral portion of a flower, often the most brightly coloured and visible part of the flower.

petiole: The stem of a leaf.

pinnate: A reference to the arrangement of leaves on a stem where the leaves appear in two rows on opposite sides of a central stem, similar to the construction of a feather.

pistil: The female member of a flower that produces seed, consisting of the ovary, the style and the stigma. A flower may have one to several separate pistils.

pistillate: A flower with female reproductive parts but no male reproductive parts.

pollen: The tiny, often powdery male reproductive microspores formed in the stamens and necessary for sexual reproduction in flowering plants.

pome: A fruit with a core, e.g., an apple or pear.

prickle: A small, sharp, spiny outgrowth from the outer surface.

raceme: A flower arrangement that has an elongated flower cluster with the flowers attached to short stalks of relatively equal length that are attached to the main central stalk.

ray flower: One of the outer, strap-shaped petals seen in members of the Composite Family. Ray flowers may surround disc flowers or may comprise the whole of the flower head; also referred to as **ray florets**.

reflexed: Bent backwards, often in reference to petals, bracts or stalks.

rhizome: An underground stem that produces roots and shoots at the nodes.

rosette: A dense cluster of basal leaves from a common underground part, often in a flattened, circular arrangement.

runner: A long, trailing or creeping stem.

saprophyte: An organism that obtains its nutrients from dead organic matter.

scape: A flowering stem, usually leafless, rising from the crown, roots or corm of a plant. Scapes can have a single or many flowers.

sepal: A leaf-like appendage that surrounds the petals of a flower. Collectively the sepals make up the calyx.

serrate: Possessing sharp, forward-pointing teeth.

sessile: Of a plant structure attached directly by its base without a stalk; opposite of "stalked."

shrub: A multi-stemmed woody plant.

simple leaf: A leaf that has a single leaf-like blade, which may be lobed or divided.

spadix: A floral spike with a fleshy or succulent axis usually enclosed in a **spathe**.

spathe: A sheathing **bract** or pair of bracts partly enclosing an **inflorescence** and especially a **spadix** on the same axis.

spike: An elongated, unbranched cluster of stalkless or nearly stalkless flowers.

spine: A thin, stiff, sharp-pointed projection.

spur: A hollow, tubular projection arising from the base of a petal or sepal, often producing nectar.

stalk: The stem supporting the leaf, flower or flower cluster.

stamen: The male member of the flower, which produces pollen; the structure typically consists of an anther and a filament.

staminate: A flower with male reproductive parts but no female reproductive parts

staminode: A sterile stamen.

standard: The uppermost petal of a typical flower in the Pea Family.

stigma: The portion of the pistil receptive to pollination; usually at the top of the style and often sticky or fuzzy.

stolon: A creeping above-ground stem capable of sending up a new plant.

style: A slender stalk connecting the stigma to the ovary in the female organ of a flower.

taproot: A stout main root that extends downward.

tendril: A slender, coiled or twisted filament with which climbing plants attach to their supports.

tepals: Petals and sepals that cannot be distinguished, one from the other.

terminal: At the top of, such as of a stem or other appendage.

terminal flower head: A flower that appears at the top of a stem, as opposed to originating from a leaf axil.

ternate: Arranged in threes, often in reference to leaf structures.

toothed: Bearing teeth or sharply angled projections along the edge.

trailing: Lying flat on the ground but not rooting.

tuber: A thick, creeping underground stem.

tubular: Hollow or cylindrical, usually in reference to a fused corolla.

umbel: A flower arrangement where the flower stalks have a common point of attachment to the stem, like the spokes of an umbrella.

unisexual: Some flowers are unisexual, having either male parts or female parts but not both. Some plants are unisexual, having either male flowers or female flowers but not both.

urn-shaped: Hollow and cylindrical or globular, contracted at the mouth; like an urn.

vacuole: A membrane-bound compartment in a plant that is typically filled with liquid and may perform various functions in the plant.

vein: A small tube that carries water, nutrients and minerals, usually referring to leaves.

viscid: Sticky, thick and gluey.

whorl: Three or more parts attached at the same point along a stem or axis, often surrounding the stem; forming a ring radiating out from a common point.

wings: Side petals that flank the keel in typical flowers of the Pea Family.

INDEX

ABOUT THE AUTHOR

Neil Jennings is an ardent hiker, photographer, and outdoorsman who loves "getting down in the dirt" pursuing his keen interest in wildflowers. For 22 years he co-owned a fly-fishing retail store in Calgary, and he has fly-fished extensively, in both fresh and saltwater, for decades. His angling pursuits usually lead him to wildflower investigations in a variety of locations. He taught fly-fishing-related courses in Calgary for over 20 years, and his photographs and writings on that subject have appeared in a number of outdoor magazines. Neil has previously written several volumes published by Rocky Mountain Books, dealing with wildflowers in western Canada, fly-fishing, and hiking venues in southern Alberta. He lives in Calgary, Alberta, with Linda, his wife of over 40 years. They spend a lot of time outdoors together chasing fish, flowers, and, as often as possible, grandchildren.